RUNNING A BUSINESS IN TIMES OF CRISIS

A business owners guide to surviving times of crisis

Edited by Kizzi Nkwocha

Running A Business In Times Of Crisis

Research: James Miller, Helen Sykes, Peter Guthridge, Mark Gregory and Shawn Willis

Edited By Kizzi Nkwocha (c)

Published in 2021 by Athena Publishing and Lovely Silks Publishing

All rights reserved. No part of this work may be reproduced or transmitted in any form or by any means, electronic or mechanical, including photocopying, recording, or by any information storage or retrieval system, without the prior written permission of the copyright owner and the publisher.

This book is presented solely for educational and entertainment purposes. The author and publisher are not offering it as legal, accounting, or other professional services advice. While best efforts have been used in preparing this book, the author and publisher make no representations or warranties of any kind and assume no liabilities of any kind with respect to the accuracy or completeness of the contents and specifically disclaim any implied warranties of merchantability or fitness of use for a particular purpose.

Neither the author nor the publisher shall be held liable or responsible to any person or entity with respect to any loss or incidental or consequential damages caused, or alleged to have been caused, directly or indirectly, by the information or programs contained herein. No warranty may be created or extended by sales representatives or written sales materials. Every company is different and the advice and strategies contained herein may not be suitable for your situation. You should always seek the services of a competent professional.

Also by Athena Publishing and Lovely Silks Publishing

Escape Your 9-5 And Do Something Amazing

Customer Service

SocMed: Social Media For Business

How To Start A Business With Little Or No Cash

Facebook For Business

Social Media Marketing: Write Up your Tweet

Getting Your Business LinkedIn

It's That Easy! Online Marketing 3.0

Business, Business, Business!

Mind Your Own Business

Insiders Know-how: Running A PR Agency

Energy Efficiency

Social PR

RUNNING A BUSINESS IN TIMES OF CRISIS

Adaptability is about the powerful difference between adapting to cope and adapting to win. --Max McKeown

"When we tackle obstacles, we find hidden reserves of courage and resilience we did not know we had. And it is only when we are faced with failure do we realize that these resources were always there within us. We only need to find them and move on with our lives." A.P.J. Abdul Kalam

"In order to succeed, people need a sense of self-efficacy, to struggle together with resilience to meet the inevitable obstacles and inequities of life." Albert Bandura

CONTRIBUTING AUTHORS

Peter Ryding, Dessy Ohanians, Karen Lambert, Sarah Lloyd, Marilyn Devonish, Gina Hollands, Clare Goodwin , Ruth Farenga, Kelly Teasdale, Dr Nancy Doyle, Darren Hockley, Jay Anderson, Rebecca McQueen, Ketan Dattani, Dr Deborah Lee and James Bell.

CONTENTS

Introduction	18
About Kizzi Nkwocha	20
How To Survive And Thrive The Corona Crisis - It's Time For Plan B!	22
Business In A Post-COVID-19 World And The Role Of AI In Reinventing Business	35
How to Promote your Business Consciously in Times of Crises	47
Marketing: How to Pivot Successfully	60
The Art and Science of Working from Home	73
Marketing Your Business	86
Making Culture Work Remotely	95
Remote Working and Managing a Remote Team	105
Creating A Happy And Productive Remote Workplace	107
Remote Management Means Managing Stress as Well as Productivity	111

Looking After your Mental Health Whilst Working Remotely	116
How To Find A Balance When Managing A Remote Team	121
Running A Business From Home And Remaining Healthy And Productive	127
Stuck At Home? From Overwhelmed & Stressed To Engaged & Connected	143
In Captivity And Isolation, We Found Freedom	159
How To Stay Creative And Keep Your Family Sane During Lockdown	169
Foods to Boost the Immune System	178

Introduction

It's an inescapable fact that there are times in life and business when we need to take a step back, breathe, slow down—and think it through more carefully than usual—especially during those rare times of national, even global crisis.

In light of present global circumstances we're experiencing, we are all being forced to navigate major changes both in our lives and in our organizations.

Many of us recognize that In order to protect our business and keep it running in the midst of a crisis, we need to do a lot of risk planning. That is the purpose of this book.

Over the coming chapters of Running A Business In Times Of Crisis you'll find valuable insight and practical advice on the steps your company should take in the event of a crisis.

It's an uncertain time with lots of unknowns, and, while we don't have all the answers, we want to share what we do know and offer guidance for our readers in order to safeguard their health and well-being as well as offering valuable advice to business owners who may be experiencing shifts in their organisations.

While we didn't choose for our lives to be upended by a global events, we can still find success by adjusting our lives and business strategies to this new world we find ourselves living in.

Kizzi Nkwocha

Publisher of Business Game Changer Magazine, The UK Newspaper, Money and Finance, The Cosmetic Surgery Magazine, Destination Uncovered and The Property Investor.

About Kizzi Nkwocha

Kizzi Nkwocha is a publicist and the publisher of Business Game Changer Magazine, Money and Finance, The UK Newspaper and The Property Investor. As a widely respected and successful media consultant Nkwocha has represented a diverse range of clients including the King of Uganda, mistresses of President Clinton, Amnesty International, Pakistani cricket captain Wasim Akram, campaign group Jubilee 2000, Dragons Den businessman, Levi Roots and world record teenage sailor, Michael Perham.

Nkwocha has also become a well-known personality on both radio and television. He has been the focus of a Channel 4 documentary on publicity and has hosted his own talk show, London Line, on Sky TV. Kizzi is the author of the book *Heavens Fire* and its sequel, *John Bryan And The Prophecy of The Popes*, is due for release in June 2021.

Follow Kizzi on Twitter: https://twitter.com/kizzinkwocha

How To Survive And Thrive The Corona Crisis - It's Time For Plan B!

This chapter will show you how to survive and thrive beyond Corona or in fact through any business crisis that you may ever face. Plus it is handbook on how to transform your business performance from good to great.

Let's face it, Corona has changed everything - your business 'Plan A' for 2020 is in shreds and your people are scared for their own and their family's lives and for their financial future. It's time for 'Plan B'.

However not everything is bad news because as a serial award winning crisis and business transformation expert I know that innovation is at the heart of business success - and change, including corona, drives innovation.

For example it is now clear that homeworking will become more common way after corona, and businesses will have to build in corporate agility into their core competencies.

If F1 teams can design and build lifesaving ventilation equipment from nothing to being used in hospitals in just two weeks, just think what you and your business can achieve in the next 12 months. Provided you adopt the right mind-sets.

And that is crucial, because in my experience 'mind-set' is the individuals equivalent to organisational culture.

And as Peter Drucker, one of the 20th century's top business gurus reported…

"Culture eats strategy for breakfast"

Of course you need strategy, otherwise you and your people end up doing the wrong things. And you need the right strategy for NOW, because what got you here won't get you there – as an individual or as a business. However culture is what brings your people together into a winning team and delivers delighted customers who become your most powerful source of new leads. So how do you get the right culture?

Well it takes analysis of what will work for your business, although there are many common threads that tend to work. However the real power of culture comes from the top. From you the CEO who not only lives the culture as a role model, you also exude the culture in everything you do. So that everyone across the whole business and into your customers and suppliers know what your business stands for? What is it's purpose? It's mission? (They are different) It's values? What it will simply not tolerate? And why are its stakeholders so proud to be associated with it?

Having saved over a dozen businesses from bankruptcy including 2 plcs and helped many more go from good to outstanding. I know that it is these things that secure any organisation's future and that skyrockets performance, profit and share price through the roof.

And because of Corona, many organisations will now be forced to dig deep to survive and then, if they choose to adopt a new mind-set, can come out the other side even more successful than they have ever been in the past.

Which is why, this article is all about how to survive and thrive through Corona or in fact through ANY crisis that your or your organisation may face.

1 How To Survive Any Crisis

The first two things to focus upon are cash and people. You can't survive without both.

1.1 Cash

We all know the phrase…

> *Sales is vanity*
> *Profit is sanity*

Fewer know the third and most important line…

Cash is reality!

It doesn't matter how profitable you are - if you run out of cash you go bankrupt! And if you don't understand your local laws about insolvent trading (e.g. when you can't pay your bills as they become due, then you must act for your creditors ahead of your shareholders and you must protect your creditors in the right order) then be aware that you can be banned as a director for 20 years, fined and even go to prison.

During a crisis its critical to become obsessed with cash especially collecting it as soon as it is due. The more any customer asks for favours or gives excuses for not paying the more likely they are to be struggling and so more likely to become a bad debt. So get your cash in on time. Also know your daily cash breakeven figures and measure it against your projected daily cash figures.

Make sure that any Business Continuity and Risk Analysis processes you use include Single Points of Failures (SPOFs) which are normally equipment, systems or people who turn out to be more valuable than the manuals suggest. I have encountered emergency power generators that had not been tested for 10 years and simply didn't work. Critical IT people such as Data Base Analysts (DBAs) who had critical systems knowledge that had never been documented and machines that made very small widgets that seemed inconsequential until you discovered those widgets were part of every assembly made in the factory and when it failed the entire production line stopped! Also when Just In time deliveries (JIT) stop arriving in time and there is no back up. I know of one clothes retail company that had dual sourced JIT clothes from China and Pakistan. However when corona first hit China in January 2020, they discovered that the cotton used in the Pakistan factory was sourced from China - so they lost most of their spring collection.

1.2 People

We all say people are our most important assets and yet few companies or CEOs really live it. And that is dangerous, especially in a crisis, because that is exactly when you need to trust your people to step up, rise to the new challenge and go that extra mile for colleagues and customers despite being scared health wise and financially.

And trust is two way, if you don't give it, you won't get it. So the question is, how do you build trust at a personal level as the CEO, and at an organisational level?

Well, of the classic '7 Cs' of trust building...

- Character
- Credibility
- Capability
- Open and clear communication
- Create a culture and environment for trust
- Congruency and clarity of purpose
- Collaborate

...my experience tells me that the first 3 make up the majority of what actually builds trust. 'Character' is about doing the right thing not the easy thing. 'Credibility' is about coming across as the thing you want to be – modelling the stated culture, living the values, and looking and sounding the part – which as a CEO in a crisis needs to convey gravitas not charisma, calm not scared, confident about the future not worried about the now.

'Capability' is about demonstrating the skills needed in the situation and importantly being seen to acquire new skills as they are needed, not just reusing old skills that you learnt a decade ago and are no longer fit for purpose. Also to role model continuous, learning as a vital mind-set for the modern world. We all have to keep learning to keep earning and actually use these new skills and technologies to remain employable. That is why learning itself is a key skill and a core competency of any modern business that wants to survive. After all the VUCA (Volatile, Uncertain, Complex and Ambiguous) world that we all live and work in means that new challenges (such as corona) will arise with increasing frequency and we must acquire new skills even faster than ever before. Which is why, instant intuitive access to bite sized knowledge nuggets has to be available to all employees 24/7. Now you don't have to provide this for yourself and your employees, it's just that if you don't, they (especially millennials) will resign and go to your competitor who does.

It's also vital that you recognise that your people are human beings not human doings and that whilst they need to be productive (even during a crisis in very unusual situations such as working from home), they also need to be shown caring, compassion and empathy. 'Empathy' being what Gandhi referred to when he said that 'Standing in someone else's shoes is not enough, rather you must walk a mile in their shoes'. Empathy goes beyond understanding how someone else feels, it is about actually feeling what they feel. Because then you make different and better decisions. And this has a double benefit because not only will you be supporting the individual person, you will be making them feel valued and special. And whilst people forget some of what you say or do, they never forget how you made them feel – good or bad. And when in a few month's time your employees are reflecting upon how you the CEO and your leadership team have acted and communicated with them over the past few months, and deciding if they stay and attract their contacts to join, or to leave and take colleagues with them to a competitor, it is their feelings that will be the biggest influencer on their decision.

So in the limited space I have in this single chapter let's move on to how do you and your business thrive through and beyond Corona.

2 How To Thrive!

For a start the biggest lever I have found in any organisation is leadership. Because when you get it right success comes easily, and when you get it wrong you and your business quickly get assigned to the career and corporate garbage bin.

Just think of football teams that are struggling and how a new manager can deliver transformational success - even with the same players. Equally the wrong manager can kill a club's success even with the same players. Manchester United is a great example of both situations.

And of course leaders should be the ultimate champion of culture which we have already discussed has a phenomenal impact, positive or negative, on morale, engagement, performance, profit, reputation and share price.

So What Is Leadership?

Well the word is derived from the old Viking word for a crack in the ice, 'Leiad' because when Viking dragon boats were returning to their home fjord after raiding European coastlines, the man at the prow of the ship had to look out for cracks in the ice to work their ship back home. As the sea ice moved so they changed the ships course. So he was called the Leiader or what we know as 'Leader'. He had a fixed destination and had to find the best route, or strategy, to get there, flexing the detail as situations changed.

Leaders are about doing the right thing versus managers who focus upon doing the thing right. And in this case the 'right thing' is less about morals (although it can be) it is about doing the most effective thing to achieve the desired result.

Which brings us to one of the key techniques all great leaders use – the 80 / 20 rule. This was discovered by the Italian economist Wilfredo Paretto who discovered that 80% of tax paid in Italy was paid by only 20% of the population. And that 80% of the 80% was paid by just 20% of the 20%. This has now been generalised as the "Paretto Principle' that 20% of the inputs deliver 80% of the value. For example 20% of your customers probably deliver 80% of your profit.

And so as a CEO you need to ensure that you know what 20% of things will deliver 80% of your organisation's future success – which will be different to the 20% of things that used to deliver 80% of your success. In the modern fast changing VUCA world what got you here won't get you there. That applies to your employees and to you! Another reason why learning has become the number one competency for every person and every business. Whilst we don't necessarily know exactly what skills we will all need in the Artificial Intelligence and Machine Learning world of tomorrow, we do know that they will be different to the skills we have now. Hence the critical need to build the competence of learning and to equip, empower and engage all employees with tools and systems to learn whatever they need to know one minute and apply it the next.

When I was a venture capitalist with 3i, which at the time was the biggest private equity and venture capital business, I developed a way of predicting whether an investment opportunity was likely to succeed or not. This was based upon extensive research into our portfolio and identified 4 strategically critical factors needed for success...

- Having a clear vison of the future
- Ensuring all key stakeholders had a compelling WIIFM (What's In It For Me) to fully contribute

- Knowing the handful of truly critical success factors each with a SMART KPI (Key Performance Indicator)
- Having and executing a professionally project managed delivery plan that planned the work and then worked the plan with an intolerance of 'distractions'.

I subsequently evolved the research into a unique methodology that I have personally used in over 200 organisations and that has delivered over £1 billion pounds of shareholder value. Including a "Strategy to Action Workshop" that has given every one of those leadership teams the exciting vision, WIIFMs, SMART KPIs and project plan that they needed to bring about extraordinary performance improvement even from what was an ordinary workforce.

Because having an exciting vision and the plan to deliver it and a leadership team that is so inspired that their passion becomes infectious across the whole organisation drives up motivation, engagement, innovation, performance, productivity and share price. And suddenly you become a magnet for new customers recommended by your existing delighted customers, top talent who want to be a part of such an exciting workplace and even suppliers, strategic partners and investors.

And when you can kick start such a virtuous circle you become like an accelerating flywheel where every rotation sucks in more contributors and more momentum to become an unstoppable force in your sector. And you personally become an unstoppable leader because people are inspired by what you do and you become a magnet for private equity who want you to inspire their portfolio, for top talent who want to be part of your winning team and for head hunters who seek you out to head up the next big thing.

I know because I have been there and done it - to businesses as the CEO and as a Chair, NED, advisor or coach to other CEOs running their businesses. It's tried, tested and proven to work both in crises and also for turning already successful businesses into even more remarkable stories and multiplying company valuations many times over.

So don't delay – start on your 'Plan B' today!

Peter Ryding

About the author

Following a high flying international career in Exxon, Mars and EMI Peter became a Venture Capitalist with 3i where he specialised in rescuing struggling businesses. He then became a specialist turnaround CEO rescuing over a dozen businesses, including 2 plcs, from bankruptcy with a 100% track record. He won the National Turnaround of the Year Award and served on the Institute For Turnaround main board.

In parallel he become one of the first Master Coaches in Europe and a Big 4 Survey found that he was one of the top coaches to CEOs in the UK. He was also Dean of Europe's leading corporate university for 4 years.

This unique blend of hard-nosed profit delivery through tough decisions, commercial nouse and inspiring leadership combined with the coaching mind-set of asking the right question at the right time to bring about personal and business transformation led to the following quote from Jeff Randall Sky and BBC Chief Business Editor…

"Peter consistently delivers transformational motivation and profit improvement, thanks to his unique combination of business and psychology."

Sir John Harvey Jones voted UK Captain of Industry of the 20th Century said of Peter…

"Peter has the special knack of getting the very best out of people. He challenges in a non threatening way and guides them to becoming the very best they and their business can be."

Peter is now on a personal mission…

"To help 20 million people, across 20 countries, achieve and celebrate more success with less stress."

…and he has created the 'VIC – your Virtual Interactive Coach' system of success to deliver the power of bite sized learning and emulated coaching to every employee throughout an organisation. And because it uses AI instead of human coaches it consistently delivers massive value 24/7 - at a fraction of traditional costs.

Peter coaches CEOs and their CXOs 1-1, is an international key note speaker on leadership and success, has written 7 books including "Houston we MAY have a problem!" was voted Top BBC interviewee of the year and runs

"Strategy to Action Workshops" for boards that are ambitious for more success.

So if you want to discover how Peter's services can help you and your organization either email him at peter@peterryding.com or go to...

https://www.linkedin.com/in/peterrydingvirtualcoaching/

VicYourCoach.com

PeterRyding.com

Business In A Post-COVID-19 World And The Role Of AI In Reinventing Business

In the famous words of Donald Rumsfeld nearly 20 years ago, we are entering a phase of "known unknowns"[1]. That is, we are aware of things we need to know, but we don't know them yet. The world of "known unknowns" is one full of assumptions we cannot validate. In business, we call this a VUCA world – an environment that is characterised as volatile, uncertain, complex and ambiguous. The concept of VUCA has been around since the end of the Cold War in the early nineties. For business leaders who usually evaluate the available information to make decisions, unprecedented events outside the organisation make this process more difficult.

The current COVID-19 situation is a perfect example of a VUCA event that is putting businesses on a crossroad to make a choice. They must choose to either 'batten down the hatches' and try to ride out the storm until the situation improves or continue pushing through these difficult times while adapting to a new world of challenges and opportunities. The problem with the first strategy is that when these businesses re-emerge into the marketplace, both the competition and the customers will have changed and 'business as usual' will no longer exist. For these businesses, the world will have moved on to a new way of operating and they will be left behind. For businesses choosing the second strategy, even today we see great opportunities to re-design their business models, internal processes, supply chains, finances, company structure and people skills. If digital services, emerging technologies and AI were 'nice to have', they are now becoming

---

[1] Donald Rumsfeld (February 12, 2002). *United States Secretary of Defense.*

essential tools for business transformation. Adoption of AI is being accelerated across different industries at a much faster rate than ever anticipated and we are already seeing amazing transformations. Such cases include:

AI In Banking And Insurance

Banking and insurance were two of the first industries to leverage the power of AI algorithms. If you have ever used a price comparison website to get an instant quote for your car or home insurance, be assured that your data was not looked at by a person. If you have ever applied for a credit card online and received an answer within seconds, the decision was most definitely computed by the bank's algorithm based on a set of criteria that determined if you were to be approved. Every time you call your bank and a computer-generated voice prompts you to say in a few words what is your call about, a programme operating on Natural Language Processing techniques is converting your words into a written command which is then understood by the computer and executed seamlessly.

AI In Medicine

In the last few weeks, we have seen the amazing capabilities of AI in medicine on the front page of many newspapers. There have been instances where algorithms have looked at chest x-rays of suspected COVID-19 patients and accurately diagnose the positive cases, in some cases faster than human doctors. In the US, AI models are used to score already confirmed cases with coronavirus and predict which ones are likely to become critical and therefore need intensive care. In Asia, the most widespread use of AI is to track and trace contacts of someone that that has been confirmed to have the virus and thus warn their close contacts to self-isolate.

AI In Retail

For a typical retailer, one of the key success factors is taking the right reordering decisions and that could entail millions of decisions per day. AI integration into the databases containing supply chain transactions can produce insights for the best and most sustainable combination of reordering stock. An example of this is ordering fresh food for supermarkets. AI algorithms can derive probabilities of demand based on geolocation, weather forecasts, demographic profiles, local events and seasonal fluctuation. This data can be then be used to make decisions that produce both profitability and sustainability. Another case of AI is with retailers that use dynamic pricing strategies where the algorithm analyses the relationship between price and demand and moves the price just the right amount. In turn, this means inventory is not left sitting on the shelves for weeks or running out before the next delivery arrives.

AI In HR

Companies that already deploy AI-powered projects in their HR practices report improvement in their data-driven decisions and improvement in employee experience as well as the more widely expected benefits of routine task automation and cost savings. With such powerful AI tools, HR departments can create personalised career strategies for each employee. When employees feel valued and their personal KPIs are aligned with their career aspirations, the company inevitably sees results in improved productivity and engagement from each employee. The second-largest impact of AI is demonstrated in talent acquisition. Many organisations deploy online forms for job applications which are then analysed by an algorithm to shortlist the most suitable and qualified candidates for the position. Given time and data, the algorithm can take this task beyond just automation and learn to 'predict' how well is the candidate likely to fit within the organisation and the level of their productivity.

AI In Marketing

Platforms like Google and Facebook have democratised the use of AI by integrating this technology in their campaign management software. Marketers are no longer required to spend time and money creating complicated customer personas and then trying to adapt their campaigns to best target them. Google can do that for you through smart bidding and sometimes with a higher success rate than the human effort. In the sales stage, AI can also be integrated into the CRM system of the company. Here, methods used by people with best conversion rates can be analysed and patterns extrapolated. A machine learning algorithm can then be trained to handle much larger volumes of enquiries and with a similar rate of success. Email and chatbots have proliferated in the last few years for this same reason.

AI In Manufacturing

One of the early adopters of AI has been companies in the manufacturing industries. The specific strand of AI utilised is RPA – Robotic Process Automation. 2020 has seen a move towards Autonomous Mobile Robots with enhanced flexibility and bigger diversity in application. What this means is that the robot can navigate an unstructured environment. This essentially means they can move around the factory while avoiding bumping into people which is only achieved due to advancements in computer vision. Interestingly, this is the underlying technology behind driverless cars and drone deliveries. As more people shop online due to local lockdown or social-distancing measures, speed of production and delivery will be essential for manufacturers in order to remain competitive. Such high demand cannot be met without some form of automation.

Myths

If some of these use cases have inspired you to consider adopting AI in your own organisation, now is the best time to start your research and preparation so that your business is ready for the post coronavirus world. But before you start, here are a few myths about AI that we need to bust so that your choices are informed by facts.

Myth 1 – My Business Does Not Need To Consider AI

AI technologies have passed the stage where they were considered just a fleeting fashion. The use of AI in larger corporations is so widespread that now in 2020 over 90% of the SME's and larger organisations polled by Gartner have already or are working on an AI strategy for their business.

In a post coronavirus world, many organisations will adopt a cost leadership strategy, i.e. compete by reducing operational costs and thus be able to reduce their prices. Even small businesses will be affected by this move and many will not be able to compete without examining and automating their processes and reducing fixed costs. AI can be one of the tools to achieve this.

Others will look at differentiation strategy where companies make their products or services more personalised to the needs of their customers. Small businesses with a few hundred customers may be able to do this using the existing resources, but even larger organisations are now able to compete on this level using AI. Suddenly, your edge of providing a unique service has been challenged by more and more players on the market.

Myth 2 – AI Can Only Replace Repetitive Jobs

One of the earliestuses of AI technologies was in the area of process automation. Process automation allows people to step away from repetitive tasks utilising programmes with predefined instructions to take over. However, AI has moved on from this basic level and has now evolved beyond improving process speeds to also include process improvements. What we are talking about here is allowing AI to bring about not only automation and speed, but a fundamental change in how to do business, aid the human decision-making process and re-design interactions between people and departments. If business leaders focus purely on automation, they will miss the opportunity to discover methods for improved personalisation and therefore improve the customer experience.

Myth 3 – Once We Implement AI – Its "Job Done!"

Unfortunately, implementing and maintaining AI systems is hard work; this is not a one-off project with a start and finish date. It is true that the beginning of AI implementation is where the work is most intense. For successful integration of AI into the business, leadership must first spend time defining which business issue they are trying to solve. AI may not be the right solution every time and it should not be implemented just because the CEO wants to have it. Here, we need to look at the culture of the company – would employees be resistant to this new initiative because they are afraid that these changes will cost them their jobs or because they don't want to trust and use the new system. Companies then need to evaluate their hardware and software systems and ensure there are budgets available for the implementation of AI. AI is never deployed as a stand-alone programme; rather, it integrates into existing enterprise infrastructure. Data preparation and data cleaning would be the next phase which consumes the most amount of resources and time from a data science, skilled workforce. And finally, the stage that is often forgotten, is the continuous maintenance of the AI system. The business environment continuously changes and that causes AI algorithms to be less accurate overtime as they become less relevant and reliable.

How to get started

Implementing AI in your business is hard work, and yet many successful companies are already doing it. In a post coronavirus world, the most innovative, agile and prepared companies will not only survive, but most likely thrive. This will be greatly determined by what these companies did to prepare themselves and how they reinvented their business models while the world was in lockdown and the economies of the world were put to sleep for a few months.

Here are a few practical steps on how to get started on your AI implementation journey:

1. **Increase your company's data science competence** – this includes both getting your data ready as well as your people. Spend this time of reduced business activity to fully audit your data – does it need collecting, cleaning or tagging, do you have enough internal data, or do you need to go and look for external data sources. The more 'good' data you have, the better results the AI models will produce. In the same way people skills can be developed internally or

externally to your organisation, you need to consider whether to upskill existing staff, to hire new competencies or to outsource certain aspects to consultants. It may have to be a combination of all three.

2. **Analyse your internal business processes**–time and effort must be dedicated to understanding in-depth how your business operates its existing processes and workflows. Then it would be a good practice to streamline the tasks so that implementing AI would be effective and efficient from the beginning. Try to reimagine your business without carrying the burdens of past decisions. You should adopt a start-up mindset as if you are starting a new company here and now and think how you would like it to operate in the current environment. This is where AI can link technological solutions with real business value.

3. **Review your employees' jobs** – with the new re-imagined business model, your employees may need upskilling, re-skilling or the business may need entirely new roles. One of the key capabilities identified last year by McKinney's' research of CEOs on skills of the future is digital inquisitiveness defined as: "A habitual inclination to question and evaluate the data before them". Employees that continuously invest time in improving their skills are better equipped to understand the insights provided by AI applications and find ways to implement them in the improvement of the business. Consider investing in an e-learning platform where employees can take courses to understand how AI could be used to improve business processes. These employees will ultimately become the AI champions throughout the organisation and inspire others to also develop the right mindset.

4. **Audit the company's existing technology and data systems**— IT is the operational backbone of any organisation. We see it even more today that without the right technology, working from home would not have been possible for many and businesses would have to close doors permanently instead of just riding the storm out. The technical

and AI skills of the people working in the IT department are key to the success of the implementation of AI applications. Historically, the primary driver for IT teams has been to protect it and secure it. Security would remain a top business priority alongside a new paradigm of democratisation of information. What that means, in practice, is to make all relevant information easily available to the right employees to be able to make data-driven decisions.
5. **Develop realistic use cases -** A useful case is a small-scale project where AI is implemented in a narrow area of the business. It is used as a pilot case to answer questions like how the work will be divided between the AI application and the employees. It provides insights on how business processes might need to change, highlights the need for new skills, facilitates the estimation of costs and benefits and, most importantly, demonstrates the business value. When ready to expand AI across the whole organisation, cases that are properly developed can help companies avoid ineffective implementation, waste resources or limit the enthusiasm forAI rollout.

These examples and tips barely scratch the surface of what is possible with the ever-increasing capabilities of AI solutions. In these early days of AI adoption, we are unable to fully calculate the return on investment of such programmes. Where we will see the earliest wins would be in cost reductions and improved efficiency but ultimately where the greatest business value will be seen is when benefits spill over into benefits like improved productivity and enhanced customer experience. Identify the company's bottlenecks and start from there, demonstrating small wins that will be the cases galvanising the rest of the organisation. Push decision making down the hierarchy of the organisation, where the information is current and solutions most potent.

Taking any step along the AI transformation journey is better than being paralysed by uncertainty and waiting for the world to return to what it was before coronavirus. That is a highly unlikely scenario. All industries are rapidly changing and any organism that doesn't change as fast the environment faces extinction.

Dessy Ohanians

About the author

Managing Director Certificate and Corporate programmes at LSBF Executive Education, CEO at the London Academy of Trading.

Dessy joined LSBF Executive Education in 2014, to define the strategy and oversee the implementation of that in the area of Professional Development, Executive Education and certificate programmes. In 2018 she also became the CEO of the London Academy of Trading. She has been an entrepreneur for over 20 years, with an extensive experience in the education industry both in the private and public sector. Dessy is deeply involved in education projects and roles alongside her positions at LSBF and LAT, being a mentor for charitable foundations and serving as governor for two London schools.

In 2017 Dessy also became a finalist in the prestigious Future Leaders Award which has come to be a platform to launch young female entrepreneurs and personalities at the early stage of their career, as well as a confirmation of their achievements and success.

How to Promote your Business Consciously in Times of Crises

'Publicity is absolutely critical. A good PR story is infinitely more effective than a front-page ad.' Richard Branson

What The Landscape Looks Like Now...

I suspect many of you have been paying close attention to the government press conferences being held by country leaders.

Regular scientific updates, on how many people have died or are being treated by the virus. Tempered with positive news stories about our healthcare heroes, educators stepping up to the plate with online courses and the latest hobbies you can take up at home to better yourself, are all flooding mainstream media.

It also shows that the media is still our window to the outside world. Even though it became somewhat skewed to a fear-based agenda.

What I see is media asking for positive news stories, feel good stories, good for our mental health stories - it just shows that things have involved in a very short space of time and there is hope for the mainstream media yet.

Whilst the situation is unprecedented, where many of us are home bound due to lockdown, there are more eyes than ever on TV programmes, online publication, news channels and social media; publicity still has its place and can still benefit businesses, if we tread with care.

In fact a recent study from Kantar asked 25,000 consumers across 30 markets how they expected to act during the coronavirus pandemic, and the top 3 strategies that came out on top included being helpful (77%, keeping consumers updated on brand reaction on the situation (75%) and being mindful (70%) (or offering a reassuring tone).

I have experienced companies pull back all together their PR efforts - this is a knee jerk fear related reaction, because in the past the first thing to go in businesses is the 'nice to have' areas – PR was always one of those.

Well people, PR is no long a nice to have – it is an essential tool to effectively communicate, connect and share inspirational stories in times of uncertainty.

Before I go any further, I want to explain a bit more about what PR is and how it can affect the customers journey.

First, what is publicity (PR) exactly?

So many people come to me asking about awareness, not quite understanding that Publicity (PR) isn't the same as marketing, advertising or social media. But just in case you didn't know PR is the art of securing coverage in the media, including but not limited to, magazines, newspapers and Radio/ TV shows.

In any purchasing decision there is a **'moment of truth'** for both the consumer and the person selling the service (the coaching 1-2-1s) or the product (the book, the cream, the mobile phone, the shoes). The moment of truth is reached through your consumer doing their research.

We are programmed to do our research. And, we are programmed to follow the crowd in some respects. And at this current time, we have plenty more time on our hands to do our research. Our mind-set is shifting. We have been told to now only go out to buy essential items only.

Fulfilment channels are needing to adapt to this new world, so online orders are taking longer to arrive at our doorsteps and online shopping slots are harder to secure.

In addition, after toilet rolls becoming like gold dust and now, we are endlessly searching for eggs, purchasing nice to have's just isn't top of the priority list currently.

The traditional customer buying journey have points in the in the cycle where the person who is buying the book, let's say for this example, will need to be made aware of it. It is through a mix of PR, advertising, marketing and social media we can help the consumer reach their moment of truth and click that buy button.

This cycle won't have changed all that much in this situation, but it is likely to take a little longer for the customer to click purchase as they come to terms with the new normal..

How A Typical Customer Finds You...

A consumer's buying journey could look something like this:

- They saw a Facebook post (*advert or PR*) about a fab new book (*recognition, but interest not piqued enough to make a purchase*).

- They see someone else they respect (*a friend or influencer*) reading said book and they have posted a pic on social media (curiosity sets in).

- They see an advert with some positive reviews about the book appear whilst scrolling on a website (*interest increasing*).

- They read about the book or you the writer in a favourite magazine or newspaper (*our person thinks it is time to buy that book and heads to Amazon to purchase said book*).

It doesn't happen exactly like this and its quite a simple example, but can you see why it pays to have a mix of awareness activities in your arsenal as a solopreneur or small business? Now that statement isn't designed to send you off into a flat spin thinking you must do everything.

You really don't. You can actually pick and choose what you decide to invest your time in. My advice here though is to try to ensure whatever mix you do select; you are mindful in what you are communicating to your audience. So, review what it is you want to share and understand a little more about what it is that could inspire others.

How Does PR Differ From Marketing And Advertising?

- **PR** is when someone else says your stuff is good.

- **Marketing** is when you say your stuff is good.

- **Advertising** is you saying your stuff is good, but you have paid for it to appear in a magazine/ TV/ social media

- **Social Media** Influencers are paid to say your stuff is good. But have to say it is an advert – i.e. they are reviewing in exchange for product or you have paid them to review. Occasionally they will review for free, but paid partnerships are more common.

- Your **social media channels** are what you use to say your stuff is good. You can use them as a business owner to share what you are doing with your friends, family, local groups, media, influencers, partner businesses. This is the place, if you achieve media coverage, you should be sharing your media coverage on. So, people can click on the link and check out what others have said about your stuff.

You need **content** for all mediums – a content framework strategy is essential: To any brand or business wanting to raise awareness and increase visibility; in these times this is where we need to be more flexible with what and how we are communicating.

Communications and **connection** are a mix of all the above. And when you are conscious in all your communications channels, and you have identified the right connections, then your essence and uniqueness shines through.

So, What Does This Look Like In Practice?

There's more that you need to know beyond how to stop the spread of the actual disease. As businesses, we need to know how to properly address this issue within our individual strategies.

We have to recognize that our PR and marketing strategies *can't* continue, business as usual, during this time.

Why?

Because, people are panicking. Their attention is not on business developments or product offerings. And if you try to interrupt their thought process with such messages, it will no doubt fall on deaf ears or even be met with a level of disdain.

Their lives have been changed and they will essentially still be getting used to that change.

The study from Kantar asked consumers how they expected to act during the coronavirus pandemic.

According to the study, 75% of respondents felt that companies should not exploit the health crisis to promote their brand. At the same time only 8% felt that companies should stop advertising altogether.

Where Does This Leave Us?

The study goes on to reveal that 77% expect brands to be helpful during this pandemic. So, we need to shift our focus from brand promotion and instead look at ways that we can genuinely help and support our audiences.

So, What Can You Do?

There are some things that you should avoid during this time, as well as some things that you can focus on until this pandemic comes to an end.

Let's consider a few of these ways you could adapt your strategy/mindset when it comes to promoting your business or sharing your story.

1. **Don't Shut Your PR Effort Down**

The worst thing you can do is shut it your PR efforts down completely. Your audience still wants and needs to hear from you.

The press still needs news stories outside of the pandemic to share with their audience.

2. **Building Connections With Media**

Like most of us, the press is also working from home, with many being furloughed over the next few weeks/months.

Many have been tasked with finding positive news stories to fill up weeklies / dailies and monthlies to keep momentum going.

So, look out for those media not covering COVID-19 – they are still out there as publications wouldn't make for much fun reading if that is all they are talking about.

Connecting with press at this time can still be challenging, especially if the journalist is home based, so calling the switchboard of the publication may not necessarily work.

When you reach out to the journalist, make sure your pitch to them is solid and relevant. Include recent examples, offer images (as photo shoots are not happening right now), make the interaction as easy and smooth as possible.

A good gauge for the type of stories being worked on and where you can help your friendly journalist out pretty quickly include channels like HARO (Help A Reporter Out – global) or Twitter (Search for #journorequests). There are also many Facebook groups where journalists are looking for help on their features so investigate groups like FeatureMe!UK. Or you could consider investing in short term for paid for platforms such as Response Source (UK).

So, This Leads Me To My Next Point.

3. **Know Your Story/Stay Relevant**

There is still a period of adjustment happening for many of us. Some of us are dealing with it differently. Some are panicking about what it means for them, in short, they are worrying about what happens next.

Try not to add to the overwhelm, stay relevant to your audience - look for ways to put your audience in first place and address their needs and concerns?

Ask Questions Like –

- How does coronavirus affect my audience?
- Have my audience's priorities changed?

- Does the coronavirus affect my product/service? If so, how can I best communicate that to my audience?

Questions like these can help to keep your audience's pain points top of mind. From here you can see what content and campaigns still apply to your audience — and which need to be put on the back burner until the dust settles.

Another way to look at this is - **are you in a unique scenario that others can learn from? are you donating / helping the community in some way?**

Can you share what you are doing in a sensitive way?

Ask yourself all the questions, I think you would be surprised in what could inspire others.

4. Read The Room – Be Conscious!

The recent study from Kantar pointed out that web browsing is up by 70% and social media usage up by 61% since the coronavirus pandemic started. This means that there are more eyeballs watching than ever before.

However, this is where you need to be conscious and sensitive in how you promote content. The virus is obviously top of everyone's priority list.

It's not the time to blast random content into everybody's social media feeds or on other outlets.

If you do, or even piggyback on the back of the pandemic, this could be triggering to some audiences and have you turn them completely off your message.

So, think about how you can best promote your content while still showing respect for the current situation.

5. **Use The Time Differently**

If your product is a low priority item, i.e. a nice to have, then you could use this time to consider other avenues to share your message.

Put any non-essential launches on hold until after lockdown – unless your product falls in the healthcare, food, technology and wellness categories.

Could you use this time as a time to slow down, rethink your strategy, rebrand, update your website, write the book, write some opinion articles.

Do all the things in your business you might not have, have had time to do.

Or, maybe even more controversially use this time to slow right down, with no guilt.

Just BE in the moment, allowing creative thought to come in.

6. **Connection Via Online Community/Offering**

If your product does fit into relevant categories, then bringing your offering online is an opportunity that should not be missed.

Create webinars that people can log into from the comfort of their home. Do a live video on Facebook, Twitter, or Instagram that will engage your audience.

Create an online community, so when you are in a position to share your product offering / service, then people are aware of the person behind. People after all buy people.

Finally, if possible, take time to produce regular videos that will benefit your strategy even after the panic dissipates.

7. Offer Your Services

Look for ways to help.

It's not all about your company. Look outward for ways to help your community, including your employees and customers who have been affected by this virus.

Whether it's with resources, technology, or skillset, ask yourself what you can do to help during this stressful time. It's not a typical approach, but this is not your typical situation.

A simple act of kindness, whether it's donating your products to a specific group, or spending time talking to people who need to hear a friendly voice, it all counts, and it feels good when we are to help.

In summary

Now is not the time to quit.

It is time to take stock and consider a different approach.

These are uncertain times, and we need to be fluid with these times.

Remember you are dealing with audiences who are somewhat discombobulated (you may even be feeling that yourself).

The most important thing in all this is to be kind to yourself and actually take the foot off the gas – if you can't do it now when will you ever!

We can afford to be thoughtful and focused at this time.

Once you have clarity on what you want to say, PR doesn't have to be pushy, but it does need to be consistent, sensitive and relevant at this time. Remember journalists are human beings too!

If you have considered all these things and you have built up your connections, you can't go far wrong.

If you are destined to share your story, then it will happen when it is supposed to.

Sarah Lloyd

About the author

Sarah Lloyd – PR Alchemist and coach – just published her first book Connecting the Dots about being more conscious in our publicity and marketing, and using the media for purpose over profit.

Sarah has been in the PR business for 25 years', promoting tech businesses at a global level – past clients included Emarsys, LG Electronics, Autodesk and Polycom. She now offers 121 services and guidance to small business owners and authors, who are looking to use PR as a means to promote their business in a way that feels good to them.

She has worked with mumprenuers, female coaches, A Fairy, a Reverend, a Swami, as well as generating awareness around festivals / wellness events.

Never a dull moment, she is also a mum of two and understands the importance of balance – in work, family and in life - after being diagnosed with PND at the peak of career. In order to get well again, she shifted gears, integrated a more intuitive approach to her service offering, and through the support of other business owners in the same situation was able to carve out a business that is successful but also enables her to be present in her own and family's life.

www.indigosoulpr.com

Marketing: How to Pivot Successfully

Plenty of companies are talking about it right now. But what is pivoting from a marketing perspective? Is it right for your business? And how can you implement it effectively? In this chapter, we explore the potential power of a pivot.

"It's not the strongest of the species that survives, not the most intelligent, but the one most adaptable to change." Unless he was even more impressive than we give him credit for, Charles Darwin probably didn't have one eye on business survival during a future pandemic when he devised his theory of evolution.

That his words resonate now is because he was describing something that should feel very familiar to every business. Life adapts. It finds a way to thrive when circumstances change. If it doesn't, extinction beckons.

How often have you read that a business needs to be 'agile'? 'Agile' as a business concept started with software developers in 2000. Yet I'd argue the broader concept of agility started rather earlier than that – because what is agile if not evolution with a glossy new sheen of corporate bells and whistles?

So as we're talking about 'pivoting' your marketing in this chapter, let's not get too hung up about that word. Pivoting may be 'a thing' right now, but it's certainly nothing new. It's one of the oldest – perhaps the oldest – concept of all: how do you know when you need to adapt to survive or thrive? And how do you do it?

In this chapter, we'll explore:

1. What is pivoting?

2. Why are businesses pivoting?

3. Why pivot your marketing?

4. How to pivot your marketing

5. How are businesses pivoting? A case study

1. What is pivoting?

I'll leave you to Google your own formal definition of pivoting. Instead, let's look at the reality. Pivoting is a change of direction. Often, it's a shift that takes something you already do or have and applies it in a different way. Pivoting can be large scale, but it doesn't have to be. IKEA building 'flat pack' homes or launching a buy back and resell scheme for used products? Both are large scale pivots on the company's traditional business model. The local pub that creates a menu overnight to keep trading as a restaurant and avoid Covid lockdown restrictions? Also a pivot, albeit on a smaller scale.

2. Why are businesses pivoting?

Pivoting happens because consumer behaviour or market trends change. Change is, of course, a constant. There has always been a need to pivot and there always will be. But the pandemic has added rocket fuel to the need for and pace of change. In one study, McKinsey found that 70% of executives said the pandemic was likely to accelerate the pace of digital transformation alone.

You don't have to look far for evidence of that. Covid has left entertainment companies reeling. All of a sudden, spending $200+ million on your latest blockbuster seems incredibly risky if you can't fill a cinema safely. In response, Disney pivoted its release model by launching Mulan not in multiplexes, as had been planned, but as a premium add-on for subscribers to its Disney+ streaming service.

Retail has been similarly decimated, and retailers have been quick to explore opportunities to pivot. John Lewis is becoming a landlord. Luxury fashion marketplace Farfetch is trialling a new live shopping platform. And on a far smaller, simpler scale, fashion retailers everywhere have expanded returns procedures and clothes quarantining, pivoting tactics to reassure customers that they can buy with confidence.

3. Why pivot your marketing?

Pivoting doesn't have to be about wholesale reinvention of what you do. It could mean changing the way you talk about it, or the audience you talk to. Not only can pivoting your marketing be extremely rewarding, it can also be far less costly and resource intensive than re-engineering great chunks of your business operations.

From a marketing perspective, pivoting typically means taking one of four routes:

> **Product:** Creating (or, more usually, adapting) a product to meet a newly identified need or extend the product's capabilities.

Customer: Positioning the company or product for a new group of customers.

Market: Extending the reach of your product by launching into new geographic territories (e.g. launching in Europe) or taking your service online.

Tactics: Changing the way you reach consumers. An example of this we'll all be familiar with right now will be the Zoom call instead of the face-to-face meeting, but it applies just as well to upping your social media presence, increasing your online ad spend or boosting your SEO.

4. How to pivot your marketing

Like marketing in general, there's no one 'right' way of pivoting. It depends on many things: your products or services, your customers, your existing marketing strategy and plenty more. But in deciding what's right for you, every business will need to consider at least some of the following:

A) Review your strategy

Covid has presented every business with a new set of challenges. For some, a slight adjustment may be all that's required to achieve a marketing strategy fit for the new world. For others, major change may be required, such as shifting from digital being just one element of the marketing mix, to it becoming the prime method of delivery.

No company has a crystal ball telling it what will happen next, so it's important the marketing strategy (like every other part of the business) doesn't stick it's head in the sand, instead staying alert to the threats and opportunities around it.

This brings us back to the theme of agility, which in practice means:

> **Monitoring:** What are your competitors doing? How are they evolving to the shifting situation? What can you learn from them, either in terms of things to do or tactics to avoid?
>
> **Measuring:** What do your metrics tell you about what needs to happen next? How is your social media engagement changing? Who's clicking but not buying? Where are the bookings falling down?
>
> **Reacting:** Even now, when it's easy to feel rather helpless in the face of the current crisis, small steps can make a big difference, especially when they benefit your customer, not just you. It's all about being helpful, which we'll get to in a moment.

B) Review the tactics

We've all found our own particular 'business as usual' challenged by coronavirus. It's important to be aware of the way things have changed for your customers too. We're all dealing with a lot of additional 'stuff', which means attention spans may be lower, stress may be higher and goodwill may be in rather short supply. That's why it's important to pivot to a series of marketing tactics that, at best, make your customers feels as though you're on their side or, at the very least, don't annoy them. Here's how to do that:

Build your brand: It's harder than ever to achieve cut-through right now - that's the point at which your message hasn't just reached the eyeballs of your reader but has sunk in and inspired them to act. It's harder still when the recipient of your communications doesn't know who you are. That's why your brand matters massively right now – because familiarity and trust are two things that can turn your marketing into a message that hits home.

That's the value of a brand and, whilst we won't explore in this piece how to build one (because that's another chapter entirely), it's vital not to make assumptions here. Yes, you're building your brand to engage new customers. But you're also doing it to maintain relationships with existing customers and bring them with you as you pivot into new territory.

Raise visibility: Now Is not the time to go into 'stealth mode'. Equally, there's little point in making a big noise in exactly the same space as your competitors, because what you say will likely get lost.

- **Be where your customers are:** In a crisis, your customers may not search you out, so you need to find them. That means a) understanding your customers' habits so you know where they are and b) engaging them on their territory. Whether that's choosing Instagram over Facebook, or a newsletter over an email, picking the right vehicles for your message matters.
- **Do more than digital:** If everyone else is on social, consider how a mailshot or a phone call may be an immediate point of difference.
- **Change the subject:** If you've grown weary of even the most well-meaning of emails that begin 'we know things are hard right now' you can bet your customers feel the same way. Find a way to change the topic, so you're still talking about things that matter, but in a less predictable way.

Customer journey: Pre-Covid, you probably knew plenty about your customers: who they were, where they were, what they wanted etc. Post-Covid, things have changed:

- **New customers:** If you've pivoted to attract new customers, then this is a new segment and a new customer journey to discover.

Take time to understand them, what they like, what they don't, where they hang out, their pain points, their behaviours. How do you do that? Analytics can take you part of the way. But user research, comments, feedback, complaints, testimonials and good old-fashioned conversation can give you the qualitative insight that really counts.

- **New journeys:** Even a familiar group of customers may be changing their behaviours to match the times. As you'll have discovered from checking the shelves of your local supermarket during lockdown, many loo roll buyers bought more, faster and earlier than they might usually. Conversely, people booking holidays have been far warier of commitment, with more research going into bookings and a high premium placed on the ability to cancel. The journey to buying changed. And the messaging required changed with it.
- **New tunes:** The ability to 'read the room' has arguably never been more important. This is about more than listening. It's the ability to hear how the tune is changing, how the mood is shifting – and then adapting what you do to show you've heard and understood. Using the example above, understanding customers is what leads a supermarket to pivot its sales messaging. Where once it might have focused on quality or price, now the mood music has changed to one of pure necessity. When the shelves are empty elsewhere, 'we have loo roll in stock now' is all the marketing message you need.

Tone: "We know times are hard right now, so how about a 2-4-1 on selected windows and doors!" No one appreciates a tin-eared approach to engagement, especially now. But hitting the right tone is about more than avoiding being borderline offensive. As a client said to me recently, "Some things just don't feel like they matter right now – we don't want to bother people." What you say needs to be relevant – but it also needs to be delivered in a way that feels authentic and human.

Be helpful: In a time of crisis, this is perhaps the most important element of all, because it builds relationships, reinforces trust and helps ensure that, once the pandemic is a distant memory, customers stay loyal. So how do you ensure your pivot makes a difference to your customer as well as yourself?

> **Product:** Think of the restaurant that becomes a takeaway or pop-up farmer's market, or the pet store that adds pet insurance to its offering.
>
> **Customer:** A great example is how supermarkets adapted opening hours during the pandemic to enable key workers or those most at risk to shop safely. On a smaller scale, online consultations for lawyers, financial advisers and private surgeons are helping to protect revenue streams whilst giving customers the service they need.
>
> **Market:** Think of every personal trainer and yoga studio that took their classes online. Or the professional membership, networking and events companies who may not have been able to deliver face to face events to protect subscriptions, but have compensated by broadening their reach and making the services they offer more easily accessible online.
>
> **Tactics:** We've seen payroll, legal and financial newsletters and blogs shift to a coronavirus focus, giving readers an expert guide through the mass of new legislation. And by using third party content those providers can reduce the workload involved in producing such material.

When you're considering how to be helpful, remember:

- Be helpful in a way that feels appropriate for your existing brand and tone of voice. The help you offer needs to feel like the right 'fit' for your brand
- Be helpful in the way you were before 2020 arrived, so it feels authentic (and so you're not seen as somehow piggy-backing on a crisis for your own advantage)
- And be helpful in a way that protects the relationship, the rapport and the trust you've built with your customers

C) Review your progress

Reviewing the effectiveness of your new measures is more important than ever right now because things are changing so fast. Schedule regular review dates to ensure you keep your ear to the ground, check what the metrics are telling you, and continue to pivot accordingly.

How are businesses pivoting? A case study

Oldham Event Centre
The Oldham Event Centre is a hospitality venue in Greater Manchester. Based at the local football club, the venue is a popular space for expos, business meetings, awards nights, weddings, parties and other celebrations. Yet as the pandemic progressed, events were cancelled and lockdown brought the traditional business model to a temporary close.

Time for a pivot. With a team of in-house chefs and a well-equipped kitchen at their disposal, the events centre switched focus. Meal boxes for local residents. Microwaveable ready meals. Afternoon tea, date night and BBQ food boxes. You name the occasion, the events centre team had a food box ready and themed for it. It proved a big success, and by targeting new customers the centre has expanded its community reach too.

The pivoting isn't done yet. Local lockdowns and the ongoing state of change means the business has to remain alert and responsive. But when the pandemic is eventually done, the centre can reasonably expect its relationship building to stand it in good stead for the future.

A final pivot

The curious thing about the sudden passion for pivoting is that there's nothing new here in terms of the *what* and *how*. What's changed for many businesses is the urgency – rarely have we needed to make such change so quickly. Rarely have we needed to educate customers at pace or bring them with us as we shift from one of way of operating to another. Yet the tools of a successful pivot are much as they always were:

- Listen and understand what your customers are telling you
- Review your current strategy
- Amend your tactics to match the strategy, taking account of your:
    - Brand
    - Visibility
    - Customer journey
    - Tone; and
    - Your potential to be helpful
- Review progress and keep pivoting

If yours is a business left blindsided by the sheer scale and pace of change forced on us all by the pandemic, it's easy to feel overwhelmed. So let's finish this section with some simple questions to help break things down into more manageable chunks that require smaller, simpler pivots.

Pivoting: 15 Questions to ask

1. How relevant is your strategy currently? What refinements should you make, if any?
2. What opportunities are presenting themselves?
3. How are you being creative in these times?
4. What new product/services are you considering that you can easily implement to meet demand?
5. What small thing can you do today that will support your future success?
6. What have you noticed about your competitor activity recently?
7. How do you plan to re-engage and excite customers about your offer?
8. How will you know you are doing the right things?
9. What's changed for your customer?
10. How strong are customer relationships right now?
11. What, if anything, would make them stop doing business with you?
12. How can you make your customer's life easier?
13. What are customers telling you – directly and indirectly with their behaviours?
14. How do you make your clients feel?
15. What if? The market is shifting. There's an opportunity to dream. Imagine your what ifs...

Karen Lambert

About the author

Karen Lambert is the owner and founder of Happy Creative, www.happy-creative.co.uk, a marketing and creative agency based in Lancashire. In her role as Chief Happy she has helped hundreds of businesses raise their visibility, build their brand, generate leads and attract customers. She is a career-long marketer with 30+ years' experience with global, national and regional brands.

She is happiest when helping others, sharing her marketing knowhow, and seeing her team and clients succeed. Karen is a keen supporter of mental health, does her best thinking in the garden, and claims chocolate makes her even happier.

The Art and Science of Working from Home

I have been a Corporate Flexible Working Implementation Consultant since 2003. This means going into organisations to implement smart, remote, and flexible working policy and strategies, and manage the psychological implications of working from home and online.

Encompassing everything from working with architects, designers, and ergonomic specialists to redesign office spaces, through to scoping and procurement of technology solutions, designing and delivering management and staff briefings, training sessions, and workshops, and offering Executive Coaching to support the mindset to transition to new ways of working.

I say an art and a science because there are several moving parts, and unseen aspects, over and above simply being at home to work.

In addition to considering the factors outlined above, there's a checklist of 45 key items I use, some of which I'll discuss here in bite-size chunks.

Boundaries

If, like the vast majority of the world you were thrust into working from home with no time to plan for it, set clear boundaries, both in terms of your working space, and your time.

Working Space

Many are working from their kitchen or dining room table or sofa. When finished working put everything away or to one side and reclaim the space; Clear away the work and reassign it as the dining room table.

Threshold

Even if working on your sofa, once you're done, get up, put your work material away or to one side, and leave the room. As you cross the threshold of the doorway, consider it the same as you would leave the office. When you walk back into the room, you are walking into your living space. Imagine arriving home. Sounds simple, however the psychological effect of not doing so can be devastating, starting with disturbed sleep patterns, and the days all blending into one when multiplied over the several days, weeks, and possibly months you find yourself in lockdown.

Boundaries With Family And Friends

You may also need to set both physical and time boundaries for family and friends, particularly if they are in covid19 lockdown with you. During the times where you are working and on a deadline, make it clear you are not to be disturbed except for emergencies, even if you are just sitting in the den. If you don't cope well with breaking your flow and concentration, also make it clear to friends the times you are not available for a chat or impromptu Facetime or Skype call.

Scope The Work

Strange as this might seem, a key problem I've come up against time and again over the past 17 years is that staff tend to over rather than under work. The problem becomes further exacerbated if the management structure is not sufficiently equipped to manage remote workers; they often then operate with a sense of fear and guilt and seek to 'prove' they are working.

Get clarity on what constitutes a full day's work with the tasks you can do from home. If the average daily output is '5 reports', when those 5 reports are complete, even if completed early, that shouldn't be a cue to do another batch unless the work hasn't been properly quantified and scoped.

There is a mathematical reason the work is often completed more quickly from home if you have the right resources, so when you're done, unless you choose to continue, you're done.

Scope The Work–Management Kpis

If you are reading this from a leadership and management perspective, scoping the work is vital in keeping track of what is being done and having a clear warning if staff will not meet targets or objectives. Periodic checking to ensure your team are both OK, and progressing will help keep the business moving if employees are not furloughed and still working.

What's Your Motivation?

If you are not a self-starter or naturally motivated, create deadlines for what you plan to do, and communicate it. If your organisation has an online portal or regular webinar meetings, state what you plan to do. If a structure isn't in place, find yourself an accountability buddy, and tell them what you plan to do by when.

It also helps to know your personal motivation strategy for the times where energy and focus are waning yet things still need to be done.

Keep Your Weekends

Unless you already work weekends, those struggling with not having a sense of structure and feel as though the days are all rolling into one, treat your weekends the same as you used to. Go as far as planning activities; it might be movie night, game day, gardening, a home facial, relaxing bath, reading, etc. Choosing activities you're not already doing during the week psychologically gives you something to look forward to, and breaks up the week.

Big Rock Tasks

I got this idea from Brian Tracy and Steven Covey. A great way to avoid procrastination. You decide at the start of the day on your Big Rock Task(s). These are the big or important tasks. This idea is you start the day with your BRTs and slot what I call the smaller 'pebbles' and sand tasks throughout the rest of the day.

Structure

If you are missing a sense of structure, create it. Even when having a lie in, be up at a certain time. Stop for your lunch break. Schedule in a herbal tea, coffee or water break, and a set finish and cut off time. If you have children, build them into the schedule, for example playtime during lunch, or set study or homework time while you do your Big Rock of or Pebble Tasks.

Connect

When I first started implementing flexible and remote working policies within Central and Local Government 17 years ago, the technology we have now did not exist; No iPads, no smart phones, no fibre optic broadband in every home and office space. Skype was around at the start of 2003.

There are so many wonderful ways to connect, so use them. When you're having a break or finished for the day, check in on family and friends. Send a text, WhatsApp, Facebook Message, email, call someone or get screen time. During lockdown and self-isolation, these small but vital human connections can make all the difference, particularly if you're not used to being on your own for long periods of time.

Get Dressed

A great way to set the tone and demarcation for the day is to get dressed. A full suit and tie might go a tad far, however your work skirt, trousers, shirt, and a tie if you prefer anchors you into work mode. From an NLP (Neuro Linguistic Programming) perspective, an anchor is a physical and mental way to access a particular state.

At the end of the working day follow your usual routine.

Move

Because the coronavirus working from home commute most likely only involves travelling between your bedroom, bathroom, kitchen, and workspace, it is important to build movement into your day.

For the past 20 years I have been prescribing my Dance Break Sessions for my Executive Coaching clients. Back then you needed to power up your Walkman or CD player, nowadays pull out your phone or head over to YouTube and choose a favourite song.

If you're fit and able to stand up and move; a simple two step is fine. If you suffer from joint problems, a chair dance will do.

If you're able to do it safely use your daily outdoor exercise break to take a walk if running or cycling isn't on the agenda.

Technology Training

I have been designing and delivering online Sessions and Workshops since 2005, and first ran meetings at the British Telecom Video Conferencing Office in London almost 30 years ago, utilising everything from using remotely recorded Teleseminars burnt onto a CD and distrubuted by post, through to various iterations of the latest Video Webinar platforms. If that thought terrifies you, get some training and learn the basics.

We've moved from a world where the progressive few were regularly working online, into a world where every man, woman and their cat and cute dog is running or attending meetings online. At the time of writing I had just logged off from another virtual birthday party.

You can no longer turn to the office technical guru to set things up for you unless you can screen share or hand your screen over, so it may be time to set up and get over any fears around technology.

Online Education and eLearning

Some organisations are no longer providing staff training because they feel staff got enough to cope with, while others would argue that is the reason training is now desperately required. If there are targets in your PDP (Personal Development Plan) or appraisal, this could be the perfect time to brush up on your skills and prepare for when the physical doors re-open.

I run everything from short online Briefing Sessions, Away-Day's and 1-3 Day Workshops, through to online Conferences and Expos, complete with Main Stage, Virtual Breakout Rooms, AI Powered Networking, and Sponsorship Booths, so remain open to what you can do online, rather than focusing on the elements you can't. You may also own what I call "shelf development" gathering dust at home due to lack of time to read or listen to it.

Team Meetings

It is important to connect with team members, either individually or as part of regular virtual team meetings. If you are self-employed start searching for related Groups on LinkedIn, Facebook, and online.

Speak Up

If you are struggling during self-isolation speak up. If your organisation has a HR Department or designated Coach, Counsellor, or First Aider, book yourself an appointment. If those roles aren't fulfilled, speak to a colleague or manager you trust. It is likely that what seems insurmountable for you just requires another perspective or alternative approach.

Change Management

As a Change Management Consultant one of my biggest tasks going into a company is to unfreeze the organisation or team, show the benefits of the change, and get buy-in for the new process or idea. It's not an easy task, because even when change is beneficial and leads to greater efficiency, profitability, or improved ways of working, people still tend to naturally resist.

If you are overly critical as you navigate your way through the coronavirus pandemic, remember we are coping with a complete shake up and threat to our health, finances, way of working, business, social interaction, and overall way of life. There may be times where the onslaught of bad news, coupled with the restriction of working from home feels overwhelming. Take heart that when you're facing a new system, even something as simple as Facebook or Instagram changing their algorithm or layout, any change to our norm can feel unsettling, so give yourself the time and space to adjust as you move through the cycle.

Push the Boundaries

In old management speak we would call this one thinking outside the box. For me, deciding to work online was a client catalyst. I received a phone call from someone who had read one of my articles in Psychologies Magazine and wanted to book a 1-Day Breakthrough Session. Great. She said she lived in Birmingham. Fantastic, and even better because there is a direct train from Birmingham to Watford Junction and London. She then paused and said: "Birmingham, Alabama."

I then paused. This was way before Coaching and Therapy was done online, and most certainly not an 8-hour Breakthrough Session, so I made a deal. I offered to do the Session by phone; Skype wasn't something everyone had back then, and if I wasn't happy with the outcome or results, I would give her a full refund.

To this day, over a decade later, it is still one of the best Breakthrough and Timeline Therapy Sessions I have ever done. I transitioned from working 99% face-to-face, to the present day which is working 90% online in terms of my Therapy and Coaching Sessions. I started running my in-person 1-3 day Workshops as live, and on-demand Video Webinar Classes in 2016. As one attendee who had experienced, both my in-person and online Workshop put it:

"I thought I would miss being in the room but this has been amazing."

Look at where you can be creative. Work with what you've got. For example, if you are a jewellery designer or have a manual craft, you could offer online tutorials, take us on a tour behind the scenes, or do A Day in the Life of Series.

If you teach a class, take that online. When I received the email a few weeks ago saying they cancelled ballet class; a hobby I took up for the first time at age 47 ½ I immediately emailed back asking if they had considered online classes. Two weeks later I received an email with not just online ballet classes, but tap, jazz, modern and contemporary. Every Thursday at 6.30pm

I now align myself in front of the camera and we all get down to our barre exercises.

If you produce food, beverages, or some kind of game, and can safely ship them, how about creating a Lockdown Basket or Goody Bag? If a couple is missing out on celebrating their Wedding Anniversary in style, show the possibility of having Scottish salmon and a bottle of champagne delivered to their doorstep.

Tens of thousands of people at this moment are being driven wild by their kids and most likely running out of ideas. Package up your Top 5 games and offer a bundle. If you developed an amazing educational App, let frazzled parents across the land know.

If you're a make-up artist, women who are used to their regular pampering sessions are crying out for expert guidance on how to tame their eyebrows, touch up their nails, control their hair, and properly moisturise their skin whilst cooped up at home at the mercy of central heating or air conditioning.

I could go on for several more pages however I think you get the idea.

Rest

A conversation I've been having a lot with my Executive Coaching clients is about also taking the time to rest, recharge, re-evaluate, or recuperate. Why? Because so many people coming into 2020 were already tired, and I don't just mean physically tired, their mind was also fatigued. If you follow my earlier suggestions around boundaries for those still working, schedule in what I call Self Care time.

What is your idea of rest and relaxation?

What do you enjoy and what brings you a sense of joy?

Who do you enjoy spending time with? Even though we are in lockdown, I will direct you back to my section on Connection.

What fun things which can be done around the house?

When did you last manage several consecutive early nights?

Closing Thoughts

My hope is this whole pandemic is soon a distant memory and we can all either pick up where we left off, or rise from this as though it were a period of reinvention, and get ourselves physically, mentally, and financially back on track with minimum disruption and lag time.

Should it drag on for several months, I hope you find these introductory tips and strategies beneficial. If you would like to book an online Consultation, Executive Coaching Session, Online Team Building Event, or Therapy Session, get in touch.

Marilyn Devonish

About the author

Marilyn Devonish, The NeuroSuccess™ Coach, has been a Flexible Working Implementation Consultant since 2003, which means going into organisations to implement smart, remote, and flexible working policy and strategies, and manage the psychological implications of working from home and online. She holds a Business Degree, Post Graduate Marketing Diploma with the Chartered Institute of Marketing, and is a Management Consultant, Prince2 Project Manager, and Change Management Specialist.

She is also a Certified Life and Executive Coach, Certified PhotoReading™ Accelerated Leaning Instructor, Certified Trainer of NLP, Keynote Speaker, Off and Online Workshop Facilitator, Freelance Writer, and Certified Multi-Disciplinary Therapist including Soul Plan Reader, Future Life Progression, Certified Trainer of Timeline Therapy, and Practitioner of EFT, DNA Theta Healing, EmoTrance, Energetic NLP, Access Consciousness, Tarot, Reiki, Archetypal Profiling, Soul Plan Core Issue Therapy, and Hawaiian Huna, having studied out in Hawaii with those from the original lineage. A Personal Trainer for Your Brain, Marilyn blends aspects of neuroscience with personal development to make accelerated performance and mindset changes more easily accessible to all, in a minimum amount of time. She has been a Coach and Therapist since October 2000.

Marilyn is also the Founder of TranceFormations™, a Coaching, Training and Consultancy organisation committed to creating impactful and lasting rapid transformation and change. Her journey into these disciplines started with being diagnosed with what they thought to be early onset Alzheimer's in her 20s and contemplating suicide in her 30s. Having found a quick, easy, and lasting way to turn that diagnosis and things around 20 years ago, she has been working with both individuals and organisations since then to help accelerate their potential and performance.

Website: https://www.tranceformationstm.com
Email: marilyn@tranceformationstm.com
Blog: https://marilyndevonish.com
Free 20-Minute Consultation: https://bookme.name/marilyndevonish
Flexible Working: https://flexibleworking.brizy.site/

Marketing Your Business

Great marketers know the act of promoting and selling products and services is an uphill struggle when taken out of the context of human relationships.

The best digital marketing channels, software and tactics in the world won't help you if your customers and potential customers don't know, like and trust you. To effectively market anything, you have to create a heartfelt connection with your audience and during times of both health and economic crisis, that connection becomes even more important. They say no one changes in a crisis, they just become more of themselves and nowhere has that been more apparent than in the marketing efforts of entrepreneurs, CEOs and brand managers in recent weeks.

I have seen people get it very right and I have seen people get it very wrong. Some were left in no doubt they had gotten it wrong courtesy of vocal critics, otherwise won't feel the true impact of their actions, or in fact inactions, until the new 'normal' establishes itself and people get to vote with their buying habits.   Make no mistake, if you are a business, expert or coach, your audience is watching right now and they will remember how you showed up during Covid-19 times for many, many years to come.

Here are my suggestions for effectively marketing through this time:

Walk your talk

If the gap between a brand's advertising and a company's actions has been narrowing for years, the current crisis has slammed that gap shut.

If you teach kindness and compassion, you'd better be demonstrating kindness and compassion. If you position yourself as the 'go-to' expert in your industry, you'd better be there when people look to you for help.

Whatever you publicly proclaim, needs to be experienced by those that come in to contact with you and your brands. There's no space for filtered Instagram accounts and hired props in a crisis. Nobody cares about your ego. They care about what's real and even more important than that, what's real for THEM.

Review existing marketing content and tactics quickly

When the world around you changes, the first thing you should do is review what you're up to with your marketing and ask yourself, 'is this appropriate right now?'

If the answer to that question is yes, great. If the answer to that question is no, pause and go back to the drawing board.

Contextual sensitivity, tone and appropriateness are crucial to great marketing and especially great marketing content.

Deal effectively with triggered audience members

We are living in challenging times. Emotions are high and tolerance levels are low, but every interaction with audience members, even the difficult ones, is an opportunity to showcase your brand or business in an increasingly better light.

'Deal with it' responses or ignoring triggered audience members is not going to help your business or business bank balance.

If one appears, acknowledge them, acknowledge that they are entitled to their opinion with compassion, apologise for perceived wrong doings, share your perspective once and once only and then move on.

Refresh your marketing strategy

Now is the time to go back to your business SWOT analysis, refresh your business Critical Success Factors and develop new marketing strategies for the medium-term.

Developing effective marketing strategies really is as easy as asking yourself: what is the challenge or opportunity presented to my business by this Critical Success Factor and how can marketing help me to deal with that challenge or opportunity? The answers will enable you to pick the marketing tactics that are right for your business at any given time and ultimately, lead you to accelerated business growth.

'Medium-term' is the key here though. There are three dominant types of marketers at play right now and all of them are playing a short-term game. There's the 'let's carry on as normal' marketers, the let's 'sell, sell, sell' and make some money fast marketers and the marketers that have let fear bring them to a grinding halt.

Our economy needs commercial transactions to take place. Stopping your marketing all together is not the right thing to do but pretending nothing has changed or aggressively promoting a 'solution' that isn't really a solution to the world's problems isn't either.

For me, this is as easy as taking off those rose-tinted glasses and realising when a product or service is a 'nice to have', or in fact, genuinely helpful within the new context we find ourselves in and then marketing it accordingly with a short-medium term view.

The longer-term view will take care of itself if you follow the rest of the guidance in this chapter and also, do not, under any circumstances, exploit fear in your marketing.

Build brand equity

Assuming your business, products and services are generating the expected emotional response in your audience, that is, they are delivering on the promise given in their key messages in the correct context, now is the time to reach out to your audience and connect with them on a deeper level, to support them and to build your reach further.

On the exit of any recession, the businesses that bounce back the fastest are those that have the most 'eyeballs' on their products and services. Those that have the largest and most loyal audiences.

Now is the time to be more visible than you ever have before. To be active on your social media handles. To ask engaging questions. To provide information and support in your groups. To add genuine value, not more noise.

If don't have automated online lead processes in place, now is also the time to get that sorted.

Make life easier for customers

First of all, do everything in your power to keep the customers that you currently have. Consider customer loyalty programmes and go out of your way to be 'of service' to them in the delivery of your products and services.

Second of all, do everything in your power to reduce friction in the customer buying journey. Coupon codes, free delivery options and payment plans should definitely not be off the table during this time.

Behave like a market leader

Brands engage, but a purpose unites. If you've always wanted to be a market leader, now is as good a time as any to step up and be one.

Leadership is based on vision, actions and behaviour not rational superiority or size. If you want to leave the current crisis in a market leading position you should be:

- Demonstrating the highest levels of ethical conduct
- Creating a future vision that resonates with your audience
- Providing momentum towards that future vision and winning hearts and minds
- Providing thought provoking analysis and opportunities to try new approaches and innovative solutions that help
- Tailoring your products and services in line with new way of working

PS - If I hear the word 'pivot' in one more Covid-19 and business discussion my head might explode. That concept is not new or specific to the current climate, it's what we should all be doing daily in response to customer feedback mechanisms. Let's not make the word or action mean something greater than it is!

Be realistic

Be realistic about how quickly you can hop from traditional to digital channels and plan accordingly.

That transition is of course possible (and indeed recommended) for a significant number of businesses right now, but even the most successful online marketers will tell you it took time for them to grow an online audience before they were able to sell in great numbers.

Analytics, analytics, analytics

Invest only in marketing tactics that meet the needs of your specific business marketing strategies and ensure that every marketing tactic you deploy has key marketing metrics in place.

Monitor the results closer than you ever have before. Anything that isn't working needs to go fast and anything that is, needs to be ramped up.

Nothing lasts forever my friend. Be human, be strategic and know that this too shall pass.

Kelly Teasdale

About the author

Kelly Teasdale is an award-winning international marketing and communications expert, business growth coach and founder of Market My Product Ltd.

After graduating from Cardiff University with a First-Class Honours Degree in English Literature, an MA in English Literature and a Postgraduate Diploma in Public Relations, Kelly began her career in London.

For over 18 years, she has worked in prominent global marketing agencies in London, Barcelona, Brussels, Paris and New York and has consulted for some of the world's best brands and businesses, including: Coca-Cola, Samsung, Johnson & Johnson, Pfizer and The Walgreens Boots Alliance.

Between 2014 and 2016, Kelly worked in-house for AstraZeneca and managed internal and external communications across various therapeutic areas and initiatives.

In 2014, Kelly gained her Accredited Diploma in Internet Marketing and successfully rounded out her traditional marketing experience with the very latest in online marketing techniques.

In 2016, she began her mission of taking big business thinking to the small business marketplace and has since become one of the most successful small business growth coaches in the UK.

In recent years, Kelly has worked with thousands of SMEs, as well as several well-loved UK brands, including The Hairy Bikers.

In 2017, Kelly co-founded *Marketing Saturday Live* alongside digital marketing expert, Matt Duggan, with the aim of making marketing accessible for small business owners in a jargon-free, practical and supportive environment. In 2019, she also launched the *My Best Year in Business* campaign to help business owners to develop the mindset, strategies and skills required to succeed.

Kelly has spoken at events world-wide and has been the recipient of several prestigious awards, including *Top 29 Under 29* (PR Week), *Young Achiever of the Year* (Communique) and the *Gold Quill Award for International Communications* (IABC).

Making Culture Work Remotely

The swift outbreak of COVID-19 meant that many businesses had to switch operations, almost overnight, from being office based to having the majority of team members working from home.

For those that weren't used to home-working, this resulted in a steep learning curve as far as technology was concerned, and also perhaps the realisation that working from home brings many advantages, such as affording team members more flexibility, avoiding distractions, saving on office costs, aiding the planet's recovery and making them a more attractive employer to future staff.

The Future Of 'The Workplace'

It is without question that business as we knew it will never wholly resume, and arguably this is a good thing. Although four-day working weeks, remote working and flexible hours are no longer a rarity, it was, before the virus struck, by no means considered normal practice.

It will be some time before we know what the working processes of the future will look like, but early indications, such as those circulating within online business networking groups, suggest that homeworking will become more commonplace. Whereas prior to COVID-19, some companies may have lacked the technological knowhow, or the operational protocol required to make homeworking default for most employees, the rapid sweep of this virus has forced the hands of many.

Despite the advantages of remote working, there are also several challenges. Amongst these is the dependence on technology, which can sometimes prove unreliable; the lag of communication when spontaneous face-to-face discussions are not an option; and, perhaps less obviously, maintaining and living the company's culture. It is this last challenge I'd like to focus on for this chapter.

The marketing company for which I serve as Commercial Director, PMW Communications, was recently placed fourth on the list of top 25 SME Culture Leaders in the UK, and as a result I was invited to speak on the panel at a business event. The subject for the panel's discussion was company culture. One of the questions from the audience was 'how could companies build and maintain an effective culture when workers were remote?' While a small number of colleagues at our organisation worked from home, most of us were based in the office, where our company culture is strong and well-established. I didn't feel I was therefore best placed to answer, and a fellow panellist took the question.

Although the event was only a few weeks ago, it was in the last 'era' of business – BC – Before COVID. I remember thinking at the time that it must indeed be extremely challenging to try and build, and live the values of, a company culture when most of the team weren't physically in one place at one time.

It's a question I've thought about a lot since the chap asked it, and a lot more since the business landscape we were so familiar with transformed into a strange new world – a world where certainty is, for now, a thing of the past, the dark shadows of not knowing loom, and yet glimmers of excitement that the future of work could – and most probably will – be even better, shine in the distance.

I even recall thinking, somewhat smugly, that this challenge the man was encountering, was one I was thankful not to have. Ah, how blissful and short-lived that ignorance was. Now, of course, it's something that almost every previously office-based business faces.

Who Cares About Culture Now Anyway?

What's that? Who cares about culture when the preservation of the company is priority? Clients are putting their accounts on pause, payments are being held back, and staff are being furloughed. Restoring those things – the bread and butter of our business – is what's important, not getting everyone slouching on bean bags and playing ping-pong, albeit virtually.

No-one could blame you if that was your first reaction. Indeed, you would be right to be concerned about these matters above all others, but denying the importance of culture at this time is perilous – no, make that possibly fatal – for businesses who intend to survive this period and come out fighting fit on the other side.

What Is Culture?

Now, there's a question. Before progressing any further, it's important, I think, to clear up what culture actually means. Culture. Crap word, isn't it? Chucked around so much by cool, cappuccino-swigging people (mainly while slouching on bean bags) it's so open to interpretation, that I'm convinced most don't know what it means. And fewer still would feel comfortable trying to define it.

If I'm going to write a whole chapter on the subject and tell you why it's so darned important, then I should at least do this. So, here goes. Deep breath.

In my words and experience, culture is a set of values that are lived (and I stress lived) by the people who work within an organisation. There. Simple. I said it, and there's not a bean bag in sight.

It could get more complex if you want to get picky about what a 'value' is, but in my experience of working at a place where values are strong and understood and lived, that's not all that necessary.

And do you know what? Our values aren't even written down. Not in a contract, not in a handbook, and not in huge text on a feature wall. We could write them down, but we don't need to because it's the human beings in our place that have formed them. Organically. Like magic. Our values are the sum of that particular group of people working for the same goals at the same time.

You can't force values. And that means you can't force culture. Sure, you can say what you'd like to achieve as a company and how you'd like to go about that. You can write on someone's objectives form that they should go the extra mile, think outside the box, and give their all to their clients with a permanent smile on their face. But if it ain't real, it's never going to happen.

Real culture comes from within. It comes from the personalities within your organisation. It's the banter, the quips, the humour, and goodness, sometimes even the brow-raising language. It's the work ethic, the gratitude for one another, the unforced praise. It's the willingness to help out, the pride in a job well done, the one who blushes, the one with the short fuse and that one, who always gets drunk at the Christmas party. And it's putting that all into a bowl, giving it a mix, and accepting that what comes out of all that is us. That's our culture. It's what makes us successful, why people choose us, and it's more powerful than a few bullet points written in a handbook that no-one ever looks at.

How Do We Keep Our Culture Going When Remote Working?

Now that we're no longer all under the same roof, how do we keep our culture going? How do we continue to celebrate us when we can no longer see and hear all that going on as often?

As at time of writing we're still relatively early on in this crisis – or should I say 'opportunity' – then I don't profess to have all the answers. However, in these few weeks alone I have learned two vital things:

1. The strength of our existing culture has helped us ride this wave

2. Our culture does not have to end because of it. In fact, there is every reason why it should flourish.

The strength of our culture as it stands has been vital in allowing us to proceed through this period with positivity. Our work ethic, collective and individual, is at the very heart of our culture, and has meant that everyone is on board with seeing this through, even when that means working longer days for less reward. An appreciation for each other's challenges has proved invaluable. We've had difficult decisions to make without the luxury of time to consider the consequences, and that has been met with understanding and compassion. A true credit to our culture. If you weren't convinced before why culture plays an imperative part in an organisation's success, then hopefully you are beginning to see the reasons now.

How does an organisation's culture flourish in this situation, and indeed beyond it if remote working does become more of a 'thing'? We are learning all the time, but here are some things we are incorporating that I'd like to share. Try them, improve upon them, then share your improved versions. In these uncertain times, one thing's for sure, and that's we're all in this together, and we'll come out in better shape if we share best practice.

Tips For Cultivating Culture In Our 'New World'

Communication, Communication, Communication

If you take one thing, just one thing, from this chapter, let it be this: if you don't take advantage of all the wonderful ways of communicating remotely that are out there so that you can converse with your colleagues, you might as well resign yourself to failure now. It's so easy, when we're deep in our own projects, to dismiss the idea of communicating with those that just weeks ago we included in our tea round. But dismiss to your peril.

Even if you absolutely refuse joining the masses and doing a Zoom call, then at least pick up the phone. The likelihood is you'll learn something that could add to your project. If you don't, then you've still achieved great things – you've had a chat with a colleague who might have benefited from your opinion, been inspired by your input or, at the very least, appreciated that you've thought about them.

Didn't BT say in the 90s it was good to talk? They were twenty-five years ahead of their time, but they were right.

If your team is a fair size, then video calls, whether it be by Zoom, Skype, Microsoft Teams, or whatever your chosen platform is, can be golden for developing work as well as cultivating culture. They can also be good for having a daily or weekly morning meeting, which gives people structure to their day and emphasis the 'team' effect.

Behold. You're About To - Learn Something New About Your People

Who knew that Sangeeta from accounts was such an introvert and actually doubled her productivity when homeworking? Or that Stu's sales figures went through the roof when he worked with a background of thrash metal?

All this weirdness we're experiencing now will bring so much to the fore that you had never guessed about your team – and in many cases, they hadn't guessed about themselves. Ask, listen, learn and gain from how individuals in your team best work, then when all this is over, consider introducing some of these things into people's days. Stu will obviously require headphones.

Bring Back The Banter

I know from speaking to people in our organisation, this is one of the things people are missing most about not being in the office. Banter (friendly, of course) is a big part of our culture, and without it, it does feel like something's lacking. But just because we're away from each other in person, doesn't mean we can't partake in a spot of humour and merry making.

Consider a departmental WhatsApp group for the more frivolous side of work or, if your culture has a tendency towards the more profound,

sentimental, thoughtful, or whatever else, then that's fine too. Giving people a platform to share finds, thoughts and funnies can help keep that all-important culture alive.

It's Not All About Work

Of course, no workplace, either office based or remote, is all fun and games, but nor is it – or should it be – solely about work. Human beings are social animals. Whether you're an introvert or extrovert will determine to what level you need social interaction, but we do all need it to an extent.

One of our more social team members had the wonderful idea last week of inviting team mates to an online video quiz night she had devised. It was a great way to bring the team together, have fun, share a few jokes and be reminded that we're all still together, even though not in the traditional sense.

Fear Not. The Future's So Bright You'll Need Shades

With everything business leaders and team members are going to learn about each other's endurance, inventiveness and ingenuity during these Corona months, there can be no doubt whatsoever that while the inevitable take-off may be bumpy, once we get up there it will be one exciting ride. If we all acknowledge the importance of culture at this time, and work to nurture it, then life will be much sweeter when we finally land.

Gina Hollands

About The Author

Gina Hollands is Commercial Director of PMW Communications Ltd, a creative marketing agency based in West Sussex. Her career in marketing and PR, which so far spans seventeen years, began following the completion of a German degree at Oxford University. She has worked across a plethora of industries from travel, leisure and retail to construction, finance and insurance.

Gina is also the author of five published contemporary works of fiction and is currently working on her sixth novel.

RUNNING A BUSINESS IN TIMES OF CRISIS: REMOTE WORKING AND MANAGING A REMOTE TEAM

One of the most challenging issues businesses face in light Covid-19 is the fact that we must embrace remote working. Businesses around the world are under pressure to restrict travel or increase the need for remote working. Over the following chapters contributors to Virus and Crisis Magazine offer their unique insight on how best to adapt to this new way of organising our business and staff.

Creating A Happy And Productive Remote Workplace

What any leader wants is for their employees to be happy and productive. However, we are now seeing increasing pressures on people's mental health and overall productivity at work. The way you, as a leader, respond to this situation, is key and should be considered mission critical.

Communicate For Integrity

Employees are being pulled in different directions, be it adjusting to working from home, caring for children or worries about elderly and vulnerable relatives or friends. All this before you consider any concerns they have over their own jobs. It is crucial for you, as a leader, to strengthen your communication with employees and show how the organisation is navigating these uncertain times. Employees will want to

hear that you are doing everything you can to figure out how to support both the business and your employees – including the most vulnerable inside and outside your organisation. Ask yourself: once this is all over, *how would I like to be remembered* as a leader and as a company?

Transparency

It may be that your company is vulnerable or at least uncertain about its future and, for example, whether you can retain all of your employees. What is key here is that you keep people informed. This does not mean revealing every detail on the balance sheet, but it does mean sharing company updates on the challenges you face, such as clients who are not paying up, as well as any new opportunities. Often companies are needing to shift focus – moving into a more brand-building and awareness phase so that when this stage passes, your profile will be high and people will choose your products or services. It is vital you communicate your strategy and bring people with you.

Why Am I Talking? (WAIT)

With people having to make quick adjustments to working from home, and with new priorities being thrust upon them, it is vital that leaders listen and allow employees the space to work through how they deal with their challenges and make the best of this period. This can sometimes feel like we are stalling. In fact, we are actually helping people 'reset', so that their next actions are in their (and the organisation's) best interests. As a coach, I help leaders regain their own productivity out of foggy, anxious or distracted times. In my coaching sessions, I am continually enlightened by the power of listening, which I emphasise with the acronym: WAIT – **W**hy **A**m **I T**alking. It is a useful question to ask yourself, particularly if your intention is to help someone.

It is very tempting to start offering people advice but often this does not 'stick'—usually because it does not address the *real* problem they are facing. They simply have not had time to express this real issue yet. However, allowing someone to solve their own problem means that they think deeply about it and 'own' the actions (so are much more likely do stick to their plans).

 Asking simple questions such as: what are you learning about this situation? What question are you asking yourself? What do you think your first step could be? What action plan could you create here? (And then stopping and really listening in between). This allows people to do their own thinking and decide the best route forward. Often our own thinking is much more powerful than someone else's advice.

As A Recap, You Should Be Asking Yourselves Two Key Questions:

1. Share your integrity – how would I like to be remembered?
2. WAIT – Why Am I Talking – to allow you to sit back, listen and allow someone to do their *own* thinking and problem solving so they can move forward.

Ruth Farenga

About The Author

Ruth Farenga, Mindfulness Trainer & Coach, Mindful Pathway offers her advice for CEOs.

Remote Management Means Managing Stress as Well as Productivity

Whilst there's certainly never been a better time – or excuse – for diving under the covers and bingeing Netflix all afternoon, the reality is that many of us need to keep working through the COVID-19 crisis. Small-to-medium businesses are having to adapt at breakneck speed to online and/or delivery-based business models.

A lot of my clients, including in key sectors like healthcare, finance, tech and emergency services are suddenly finding themselves in hastily-organised remote working situations. Suddenly, the structure of office on site life and support networks are being replaced by conference calls and daily uncertainties as to what 'best practice' means now.

None of us can predict how long or how bad this crisis is going to be, and this new reality will be tougher on some colleagues than others. There are psychological factors to consider for those who are suddenly required to work remotely. Myself and my team of trainers are currently advising employers (remotely, via webinar) on how to adjust during this crisis to reduce stress and productivity difficulties. Based on that advice, here are some of our suggestions to help managers and their teams to adjust to the new working landscape.

We're All In This Together – Doing Your Best Remotely

Lay out your working plan for everyone as clearly as you can. It's a good idea to acknowledge from the off that the new working methods are unlikely to be plain sailing initially. Getting used to things – from getting everyone to mute their mic on Zoom to new complaints protocols – is going to take time.

Not all colleagues will have the same level of ease with virtual comms. If you have any staff with neurological differences this is particularly important. There are going to be points missed and/or lost in translation. Be patient and emphasise the importance of good communication over 'getting it right, first time'.

Well-being Is Paramount

Within every workforce, there are always going to be some colleagues that handle change better than others. For some, the rate of change during the COVID-19 crisis has been overwhelming. Working with the neurologically diverse means we are familiar with anxiety and stress triggering safety-seeking behaviours. Anxiety can manifest in a number of ways, and is known to be higher for home workers, as the boundaries between home and work get blurred, affecting the amount of 'down time'. One thing to look out for is colleagues who 'cope' with the new environment by becoming fixated on work as it morphs into their main connection to 'normality' and the outside world. Make sure you and your staff stick to allotted working hours and put in place some ground rules for those working unsociable hours to accommodate their home life, such as out of office autoresponders and rules around social media contact.

Take Time Out

Make sure your colleagues take lunch and screen breaks. And, if they're not self-isolating, encourage staff to get some exercise and fresh air. Having some non-work-related chat-time is also a good idea, enabling us to check in on everyone's state-of-mind, managers included. You may want to consider scheduling regular wellness workshops. If your organisation has the scale, a workplace well-being psychologist might be a worthwhile investment. They could host webinars where people can share their anxieties, with a positive focus on exercising the control we do have over our situation. Getting ahead of this before people become fatigued or overwhelmed will be key, starting the conversation and giving people time to express themselves will add a layer of support.

No One Left Behind

Connectivity within teams is going to be crucial for maintaining the group energy and innovation that is needed to get through these challenging times. Your team members are all stakeholders in making this new emergency situation work. Make sure you include everyone – even the quiet ones – in group conversations. There will likely be unexpected problem-solving and improvements to your workflow happening now that will carry through when the quarantine is lifted.

My Family And Other Animals

Many workers will be doubling up as carers for older and younger dependents also on lock down. Suggest, if possible, a designated work area to help create a physical border of sorts between work and home. It won't stop the cat walking on the keyboard during conference calls, but it will give everyone else in the household clearer boundaries during working time. And accept that for some, this is going to be a serious compromise. Full time caring and full time working is not possible for the long haul – see what accommodations you and the rest of your team can make, some human kindness and sharing of workload will translate into serious loyalty and appreciation down the line.

The World Transformed

As is often the case with seismic shifts of this magnitude, when we emerge from this pandemic, we won't be going back to 'normal'. Our societal structures and safety nets are being stress tested like never before. We will look back on this as a pivotal moment in how we organise our institutions. Let's apply what we already know from solid psychological research to support our colleagues to work at their best in more flexible and resilient practices that can remain in place for those who benefit. People with caring responsibilities and disabilities have been requesting greater access to flexible working for a long time; it will be much easier to implement after this! Necessity is the mother of invention, as the saying goes.

Genius Within's daily webinars for managers draw on evidence-based research and guidance on best practice for managers supporting remote workers, including the psychology of working online, mitigating isolation, creating momentum and energy and communication etiquette. If you are a key worker, these courses are free.

Dr Nancy Doyle

About the author

Dr Nancy Doyle is a registered occupational psychologist with 15 years' experience of assessing and coaching neurodiversity at work. She campaigns with the British Psychological Society and is a Research Fellow at Birkbeck College, University of London. Nancy is the founder and CEO of Genius Within.

Looking After your Mental Health Whilst Working Remotely

For so many of us, our working life is rooted in human interaction. We're used to offices filled with the noise of phone calls, meetings, and chatter. Our colleagues are often hosting business meetings, or else off out to meet clients and associates themselves.

Although, it's possible that prior to the COVID-19 outbreak, some of us were used to working from home the odd day here and there – or even more than that – being forced to do so in the midst of an infectious outbreak can still feel daunting.

As business leaders, it's our job to take this into consideration alongside the wellbeing of our employees. We should take steps to support and manage the mental health and morale of our teams as we navigate this uncertain terrain.

A New Challenge

Like many others, our business has undertaken a swift switch to online communications during the government advised social distancing. Using comms tools such as Skype, Slack, or Microsoft Teams, or task management software like Asana, Trello, and Hubstaff, we've managed to keep in touch with one another and keep the work flowing.

Still, separated from our usually vibrant teams, many employees are at risk of feeling lonely or isolated right now.

As well as being bad news for the mental wellbeing of staff, over time, isolation can cause employees to feel disconnected from the company and its larger goals.

To mitigate this risk, below are some easily actionable tips to aid boosting morale and productivity for businesses during this time:

Stay Focused

Rightly or wrongly, many business leaders are concerned about productivity whenever staff work from home. This is particularly true for firms where it's not the norm. However, the good news is, you can prove the stereotype wrong!

Ultimately, your accomplishments during this time will speak for themselves (however you track them, be it billing figures, hours logged, projects completed, and so on), so staying focused is key as staff continue to self-isolate.

At the moment, one of the biggest distractions you'll face is the news. Checking for COVID-19 updates, or clicking on alerts as and when they pop up, is going to be hard to resist.

Employees should be wary of scrolling themselves into despair, however. Relying on unreputable sources for news about the outbreak can fuel anxiety, making it difficult to concentrate and putting your wellbeing at risk.

Remember, many news sources rely on click-bait and scaremongering for views, so schedule "news breaks" – maybe 1 or 2 a day – and stick to them. Turn off news alerts and choose your outlets carefully, ensuring they are quality sources (try Gov.uk or the World Health Organisation).

Inspire Your Team

During times of global business disruption, it can be easy to feel concerned and uncertain about the future. Your employees may feel overwhelmed or worry that there's 'no point even trying' to meet their goals.

It's your job to maintain momentum during these instances, so communicate updates frequently and offer positive feedback. This is one of the best ways to inspire and motivate your team (and it will help you to keep forward thinking too).

Keep the future bright by sharing your plans; ensuring employees are 'in the business loop' will mean they're far more likely to work with you as you implement business continuity plans.

Communicate Effectively

Communicating effectively whilst away from the office is suddenly *very* important for businesses, and especially for managers with a team to support.

Remember, video calls are far more effective than email and even phone calls when it comes to avoiding miscommunication – video chat is a way to humanise virtual communication.

Seeing your employees and clients face-to-face in this way is important, as it allows you to pick up non-verbal communications and character cues, e.g. their environment, facial movements, and clothes.

These aren't things anyone would think to email you about, but they allow you to get to know people better, in an intuitive way, and make judgement calls.

Maintain A Work/Life Balance

For staff used to going into the office, blurring the lines between work and home can feel stressful.

There's suddenly no need to dress smartly or stick to a routine, and even the lack of commute (a time we use to enter into one mindset or another) can mean it's hard to switch off at the end of the day.

Sadly, this can mean bad things for mental health.

Since many businesses will be so reliant upon online communication during this period, it's going to be very important to 'go off grid' after your workday is complete. Try to stay offline and relax in other ways, e.g. cooking, watching a movie, or reading a book.

Another tip is to integrate a 'transition' period between work and leisure time – a sort of symbolic commute, if you will.

Perhaps you will walk the dog every day at 5pm, search the internet for a new recipe to try, or enjoy a bath. Whatever it is, developing this habit over time will signal the end of the working day for you, helping to begin your evening wind-down and maintain your wellbeing.

Darren Hockley

About the author

Darren Hockley is MD at DeltaNet International. The company specialises in creating engaging compliance and health and safety e-learning for businesses around the globe, including training on remote working.

How To Find A Balance When Managing A Remote Team

It's no secret that the world is in a unique situation right now as Covid-19 continues to escalate across the UK and globally creating new challenges for businesses we have never witnessed on this scale before. The majority of office spaces have been closed for a week now and for many people this could be the state of play for the next couple of months, but how individual workers react to these new changes will no doubt vary drastically.

For managers, it's all about finding a balance between trusting your staff but ensuring that work continues to be completed to the same high standards you would expect during normal business function. You don't want to appear micro managerial but you want to maximise efficiency where you can.

Here, James Bell, customer experience and production director at Mitrefinch, provides some practical tips for employers on how to manage remote teams most effectively.

Communication is critical

Streamlining the use of software is often key to effective communication and helping to ensure no members of the team miss any vital information. The easiest way to do this is to agree with your team on the core methods of comms and ensure everyone sticks to this for core business discussions. At a time where you have the added barrier of not being in the same physical location, using one programme alone mitigates the risk of messages getting lost in the ether.

And, while regular contact should continue as usual through email, internal messaging (or whichever platform you typically use on a day-to-day basis), phone calls and video chats are critical at the moment. Not only will a friendly face-to-face talk be welcome during this time of self isolation, it also helps staff to feel they're not alone and ensure any potential miscommunication through text is minimised.

In situations where particular employees need to be on certain calls or video meetings, make the relevant parties aware well in advance and ensure that their calendars are updated to reflect this; when working from home, it can be easy to lose track of important calls and upcoming meetings, but you can prevent this by making use of a shared calendar system.

Outlining all of this in one central document can ensure all of your employees are on the same wavelength and ensure staff are using the correct lines of communication and are responding correctly to internal and external enquiries.

Set expectations and manage tasks

Once all staff are aware of upcoming meetings or calls and using the same means of communication, managers will find it much less complicated to monitor the progress of tasks whilst remote working. Using streamlines methods of communication, staff will be able to check in with each other on a regular basis to ensure tasks are on track as planned without appearing overbearing from management.

Project management platforms, when used correctly, can also be a great way of managing workflow across teams to ensure work is completed on time and that tasks are shared fairly and evenly.

Instruct your employees to continue updating the status of tasks as they would under normal conditions; issues can arise when a staff member neglects to keep others up to date with a piece of work when working from home, particularly with projects that involve sequential tasks and multiple employees.

It is now even more important that managers are clear with setting objectives and timeframes in which work is to be completed and to keep staff engaged throughout the process and when a task is completed. For example, public recognition through an instant messaging system or social media can help employees to feel a sense of achievement when they have completed a particular piece of work.

Don't let remote working limit your ability to collaborate

Team members can easily move about to facilitate collaborative work within a physical office, however this doesn't need to stop when teams operate remotely. With the entire workforce cooped up in their homes, they may begin to feel isolated so collaboration at this time is more critical than ever.

But, this only works well if staff are encouraged to reach out to each other through conference calls or video chats. It's a good idea for management to instigate such collaborative sessions from the outset to get the ball rolling, then contact employees on a regular basis to ensure that they are still taking place.

It is therefore essential that all members of staff have easy remote access to any data and documents that they may need and that adequate security measures are in place to mitigate the risk of breaches.

Ensure that some form of file-sharing system is in place and accessible to everyone before the remote working period begins – this is where brands should utilise cloud-based hosting where possible.

By James Bell

About the author

James Bell, customer experience and production director at *Mitrefinch*. Mitrefinch is a global provider of integrated Time & Attendance, Payroll, HR and Access Control solutions. The company has designed user-friendly and cutting-edge products that help organisations increase productivity, profitability and manage their workforce effectively.

Running a Business in Times of Crisis: Your Health and Well-Being

Running A Business From Home And Remaining Healthy And Productive

Running a business has its challenges at the best of times. Navigating through a crisis like a pandemic adds challenges that none of us could really be prepared for, especially for a business like Body & Spirit, which is based on face-to-face interactions between clients.

Once it became clear that social distancing would be important to help stop the spread of COVID-19, it was important that we adapted quickly so that we could continue to offer our core services. In addition, with myself and our team members all having young families at home to care for – and no formal childcare in place anymore – it was important to find an entirely new structure that would provide a balance between work and family life.

On top of everything else, I was very concerned that all of the hard work I had put into my own mental and emotional health was about to go out of the window through a shear lack of space and time. I was definitely feeling the fear on many levels!

Body & Spirit Before Coronavirus

At Body & Spirit our aim is to provide physical movement, mind-ful activity and spiritual practices that support people on their personal journey to health and happiness. One of the core values we hold is 'support' – for our clients, the wider community, and our team.

We want to support our clients on their own path of development and discovery. This has always been a very hands-on interaction; allowing strong connections to develop.

It is also important that we are there for each other behind the scenes. Through group interaction and easy communication, everyone from office workers to support workers, teachers and therapists, should have what they need to work happily and effectively, within their own work-life framework.

For our team I aim to allow, and facilitate where possible, each person to support themselves. Whether that be through continued personal development courses or supporting the balance of time at work with family needs.

The harmony of these three has always been fundamental to the running of Body & Spirit. Before even setting up the company, I wanted to be able to offer clients what they needed while managing my own needs for personal growth and time with my family. This was something I had previously found – and sometimes continue to find – very difficult. I was keen that going forwards, new team members coming on board would feel strongly about offering the best they could to our clients, while being able to have their own work-life balance needs met.

One of the other values dear to my heart is providing a polished service. I wanted the experience of coming to Body & Spirit to be easy; to be high quality and to feel genuine and personal. Until the coronavirus crisis began, this had always been achieved through a close 'hands on' approach. Both physically, using hands to guide the body itself, and emotionally, creating open channels of communication during, and in between face to face sessions.

Working Through A Pandemic

Now suddenly, the world had changed in a day and people were no longer able to have contact with each other. Continuing to run such a hands-on business was going to be a huge challenge.

No longer could I have a physical connection with my clients, and yet potentially, the sudden and unexpected change in the world meant they may need their classes and therapies now more than ever. My beautiful childminder – who is like a second Mum to my four-year-old – our fabulous babysitter, and amazing nursery school teachers, who had all been instrumental in helping with our beautiful daughter (it takes a village, right?!), were no longer there to help. I was completely unable to connect face to face with the incredible team I was slowly building within and around Body & Spirit. And, I was also keenly aware that not only was my business in jeopardy, but if I was unable to pay others for their help, their businesses and incomes were at risk too.

I was faced with having to completely rethink the entire way I worked, make the seemingly huge changes necessary to keep Body & Spirit running, and figure out how, between my husband and I, how we could work fulltime jobs and be fulltime parents to our daughter.

My brilliant marketing manager and assistant, who I rely on to help me 'hold all the balls in the air', was in the same boat. She was trying to retain her business while her husband continued working outside of the home in a key worker role, and also looking after a two-year-old – with no additional daytime childcare. I needed her yet I wasn't sure I could afford her anymore, or that she could work in quite the same way.

Coping In A Crisis

The first three weeks of the virus threw up completely different experiences, with each week requiring very different energies, decisions and strategies. I was experiencing a rollercoaster of emotions for sure.

Week one felt really tough. It was to be the 'doing and worrying' week. I was concerned for the health and wellbeing of our clients as they went through what was to be a very difficult time, and for the ability of Body & Spirit to cope financially.

For many different reasons, from concern about infection to their own financial uncertainties, some clients were making the decision to stop taking sessions for a while. Others were wanting guidance and certainty in the ability of their sessions to provide what they needed, while keeping safe and healthy.

Within that first week, I made the decision to take the entire business online, keeping all classes running and even developing some new ones. I have to admit, I was sceptical that working from home in this way could be as effective. I wouldn't be able to just reach into the screen and be hands on. I know some clients had their reservations too, but I am happy to say, those who were unsure at first adapted quickly to our new way of working. I was particularly surprised at the effectiveness of sessions with private clients, where it was sometimes even easier to see via our online interactions what was going on within people's energy and bodies. I also had great feedback from clients who were equally surprised at how much they were enjoying their sessions and how grateful they were to be able to continue to keep themselves happy and healthy. I know that across the country and the world, many businesses were moving, online and I am sure this will be forever known as the time of 'Zoom'!

However, for me, this was not enough. I felt strongly that further plans and strategies were needed in order to maintain the supportive and polished service Body & Spirit offers.

Up until now a strong website had not been high on my list of priorities as there was always so much else to do. Now it has become an invaluable resource. My amazing husband (the creative and techy one of us) swiftly developed the existing small landing page into an amazing place where people could find lots of information. An extra 'resources' page was included with tips on using Zoom effectively, finding music and equipment that could be used at home during online classes, and offering short videos that could be used between sessions – to help with the inevitable aches and pains created by working from home and living in a stressful time.

As information from the government was ever changing, I also began publishing videos, emails and social media posts with regular updates. I wanted to be present and to bring clarity in uncertain times. This kind of work was something I had always avoided, partly for fear of bombarding people with information and partly for fear of not doing it well enough – or not looking as good as others! Suddenly none of this seemed to matter. Everyone trying to maintain a business was in the same position. We needed to be able to support our clients and customers, and few were able to have luxurious or beautiful backdrops, makeup artists and hairstylists to create a stunning video. Freed from these irrational fears, I was surprised at how producing extra content, or as I like to see it, 'using my voice', wasn't as bad as I expected. I still don't love this kind of work; it's why I am a teacher and guide, and not in marketing, but running a business requires both, and a fear has been lifted – a little.

I was also very keen to personally call or connect with as many individual clients as possible, particularly those that I would not now see for a while. For some it was important that this happened within the immediate 24 to 48 hours of that first week, for others it would be something I would do over the course of the coming weeks. I wanted to simply chat, check on how they were doing and to discuss any questions or concerns they may have had. This was time consuming but was very well received.

Finally, I dearly wished to be able to help those who were not our clients and needed support too. The idea to offer free online meditations to anyone was almost instant. These were broadcast live on social media most days of the week, at a time that helped people develop a good daily routine and recorded for those needing them at a different time. Again, the feedback was great. I was in tears reading some of the short messages I received from people who I had never met before telling me how the meditations were helping support them through a very challenging time.

****

After the initial explosion of activity (and sleep deprivation), weeks two and three bought about very different challenges.

As things became a little less hectic, I had some time to think. In many ways this was harder. The fears began to surface. I wasn't yet finished with building the Body & Spirit dream and yet it may all come tumbling down. How would our family cope? What would be the effect on my own mental health? And of course, could I bring in enough money, and would the business survive financially?

I experienced the emotional tug-of- war between shrinking, ceasing to pay for everything and everyone bar the absolute basic essentials, and – thinking abundantly – knowing that if I could continue to run the business as fully as possible and to continue to pay for as much as was sensible, I could sustain Body & Spirit and maybe even flourish.

In the end, slowly and inevitably some of the basic decisions were taken by the government and, as things shut down nationally for our initial lockdown period, I was no longer able to use studios, or to take unnecessary journeys – let alone make face to face contact with anyone outside my household. This clarity made many of the decisions simple. However, I still felt inner turmoil about how to continue working with other practitioners and businesses. I did need them, but could I afford them?

Throughout my adult life, I have struggled to step away from feeling small and restricted, or to see my worth. I had, and still do have, a fiercely strong work ethic – of which I am proud and give thanks to my amazing parents for.

However, I could never quite seem to find a work-life balance, my purpose, or real happiness. I wasn't even sure what those things looked like. Life felt like a lot of hard work for small reward and something had always prevented me from really growing and discovering. In recent years however, my body began to give me great big signs that things were really not working. It was then that I embarked on a personal journey of discovery and growth. Along the way, life introduced me to the 'right' people with whom I developed some important and supportive relationships for which I will always be grateful. One of these was the work undertaken with an energy healer, and another with a like-minded business coach – both of whom are so much more than their titles suggest. Along with close friends and colleagues, they have helped immeasurably with my personal and business journeys. These connections have allowed me to understand myself better, to truly see who I am, what I am good at and what I want to offer. These were the people who had really helped me and my business to flourish.

And yet, at a time of real crisis these were some of the people I was considering pushing away because I wanted to hold onto the money I had. Through conversations with them, others and myself, I was reminded that health and growth can only come when you continue to invest (however that looks) in yourself. I was reminded to always ask the questions: are you making this decision out of fear or abundance? What do you want to achieve in this time? And, how do you want to be remembered after this time? Realisation also dawned that the connections I had with these people were the same connections I had with my clients. Whilst Body & Spirit may not be a front-line service, people would need what I offered, now and especially in the future. I wanted to be able to continue to work with and support my clients, and I knew that my healer and coach wanted to continue to support me.

Daily I changed my mind as to whether I could bring myself to take a leap, spend if I sensibly could, and think abundantly. At the time the decision seemed hard. Looking back, I am grateful I chose what seemed like the more difficult path. Spending and growing when many were hunkering down. The choices I made here completely changed the course of my life through the coronavirus outbreak and, without others, I may well have trodden a different path.

****

In terms of balancing home life with the demands of work, it took a little longer than a week, or even two, to develop a private routine that allowed our household to function, to remain sane and stay healthy. Important conversations were necessary; from the 'money talk' to 'this is what I need talk'.

On a practical level it became increasingly clear that we needed a 'how to live and work at home, and not kill each other' strategy. I needed to use different rooms for different jobs. The living room was the only room big enough to teach a class in, but this meant kicking the family out. For the meditations I needed a space where I would not have a four-year-old coming in to ask for help on the toilet! The kitchen became my husband's office – not ideal, and the dining chairs were not helping his neck – or mood!

There was so much to do that the easy road was; working, begrudgingly finding time to play, shouting at each other, letting the stress build up and never leaving the house. We had to talk; about family time, getting out of the house and money worries – and we needed to order Daddy a proper office chair!

We developed a schedule of who was working where and when. During working days, even though we were under one roof, my husband and I became a bit like ships passing in the night, one working while one was doing family time and then swapping. Of course, we had to work within the obvious constraints; I had to be teaching at the times classes were needed, and my husband had to be at his desk and online during traditional office hours. We sat with a pen and paper and worked out a schedule. This worked well, but no matter how well we planned, there were always going to be those times when we both needed to be in meetings and classes at the same time. Our daughter became famous on her Daddy's Zoom meetings and I am not ashamed to say that 'Nanny iPad' certainly played a role!

As a balance to this weekly schedule, it was obvious that taking complete time out for the family, and for ourselves, was going to be really important for both physical and mental health. In one small respect we were lucky that all of this was happening during a beautiful blooming springtime. Having the garden as an extra 'room' on the house was heaven sent. So, organising personal time on paper was fairly straightforward; scheduled walks, proper days off and planned individual activities (now all online of course). The greatest challenge I found with this was the mental switch between work, family and me time. I have always found this difficult anyway, but usually there is travel between work and home, and time to gently transition your headspace. Now time between things and away from each other was gone. For me there was – and still is – no easy fix for this. I still find myself thinking about one thing when I am doing another or struggling with the switch of pace between different activities. This is stressful, especially when deadlines loom. I particularly worry about the, "I'll be with you in just a minute," that my daughter hears far too often, and I have had to accept that sometimes, things just take longer than I would like. It's easy to think that everyone else has it sorted, but this is my story to live, I can only do what I can, and I know I am not superhuman. So, I try to give myself a break.

*****

Speaking of which... For our relationship, my husband and I had to have two important conversations. How could we give each other a break, and how we would manage our finances? Otherwise, we may well have been taking a permanent break! I have heard it joked that with everyone living in such close quarters together, it is the divorce lawyers who will be coming out of this time most well off!

Firstly, we needed to give each other the time to do the things that sustain us as happy humans. For me that was taking time with my spiritual and physical practices, for him, tinkering with his car and bashing his drum kit (I am sure the neighbours are glad for muting pads!). For both of us together it was time spent working and playing in the garden.

Secondly, we needed to have 'the money talk'. How much did we have? How much were we likely to earn in this time? What were our priorities and what could we live without? How could we pool our resources differently from normal if needed? We also found that this was not a one-time conversation. As the situation changed over the weeks, both nationally and personally, we were to repeat this discussion on a couple of occasions.

****

Finally, having worked out the finances, and having faced the spending fears, I knew I needed to continue to work with my assistant if I could. Thankfully, due to the values that Body & Spirit holds, we already had a good foundation. We knew what each other needed, what personal boundaries were in place and what the work-life balance looked like for each other (usually meaning that something would always take longer than expected on my part!). All we really needed to do was look at any specifics that needed change. I set in motion weekly catch up meetings. Not too long, just enough time to check in on how she was doing in herself, where we were at with current jobs, new ideas and innovations, what needed to be done going forwards, and if we both had the tools and support required to do the job at hand. We also changed our 'available to work' hours in light of our new home situations. The structure and boundaries put in place gave us confidence in what we were doing and personally, allowed me to turn my head off when not in those 'working hours'.

Moving Forwards

There are going to be many more challenges in front of us I am sure – already things are changing in the world again. The transition from life now, to the new life awaiting us all is going to be long and will, I am sure, require continued innovation and renewed perspectives. It may be even harder as we all go through many gradual and subtle changes and the government guidelines are inevitably less utilitarian and absolute.

For Body & Spirit, it has been incredibly difficult at times, but the changes have taught me a lot; about myself, about the things I can and want to achieve and about the things I want the company to offer. I am sure that many of the changes made in recent weeks will remain and I can see the potential for some new and exciting developments on the horizon that I never would have expected. Knowing that we have adapted and innovated so well gives me confidence that we can see our way through the road ahead.

In many ways the fear now is of going back. So much sadness and difficulty has been experienced and endured by so many, and none of us would have wished this on anyone. I only hope that going forwards we can, all of us, continue to support each other, take care of the world around us, and make decisions with love, not fear, greed or selfishness.

Gratitude

I hope that some of the ideas and stories here are helpful. I have certainly not been able to devise and do all of this on my own. Never have I been more aware of the amazing people I have around me or more grateful for their own individual gifts.

To those of you joining classes, sessions and meditations: I would like to say a big thank you for all of the fantastic feedback and continued support. It has been a pleasure to work with you. To the amazing people in and around Body & Spirit, your ideas, feedback and support has been invaluable. You may not have always had the same point of view, but you have all held up the mirror and given me the sounding board I needed to flourish and grow in a time that could have been so different. Finally, to my family and friends, I could not do what I do without your love, support and very often practical and unpaid assistance. I love and cherish you all.

Clare Goodwin

About the author

Clare Goodwin is founder of **Body & Spirit**, which provides classes, workshops and retreats to support people on their journey to health, happiness, and a better quality of life. Clare's work is firmly rooted in the understanding that everything is connected; body, mind, and spirit.

Clare began her working life as a professional dancer, before becoming a personal trainer. However, the fitness arena felt restrictive, and she became more aware of the need to work with people on strengthening and improving their bodies in a more holistic way. Through discovering the practice of Pilates, Clare's world opened up. She was able to help people get stronger and fitter, improve postural balance and functional ability, and get rid of aches and pains that had plagued them for years.

Over the coming years Clare was diagnosed with Type 1 diabetes, married the love of her life, made the big move from London to the country, and had her beautiful daughter. She loved her life but despite preaching it, wasn't always happy or healthy.

At this point she embarked on a slow and gradual journey of learning and personal development. From discovering the power of meditation to understanding her moon and menstrual cycle, to discovering personality patterning, finding the chakra, hara line and core, this whole new world strongly informed the way Clare wanted to work.

By including this deeper mental and emotional approach, her Pilates classes have expanded and developed. She has found a passion for the incredible results of Yamuna Body Rolling, and meditation now plays an important role as a stand-alone offering, and as part of physical classes and workshops. Her calling is in helping people on their own personal journey to health and happiness with a particular gift of focusing on the body, how it can communicate with you and tell you what it needs.

To find out more about Clare & Body & Spirit visit:

http://www.clare-goodwin.com/

Stuck At Home? From Overwhelmed & Stressed To Engaged & Connected

Abstract - The challenges of being stuck at home with everyone... "From overwhelmed & stressed to engaged and connected". Helping the whole family to get along better. A Psychologists perspective on improving family dynamics... The strength of the parent-child relationship and the cohesiveness of the couple relationship - both in intimacy and in shared parenting. This chapter considers some of the challenges and offers practical suggestions for improving things together at home.

A worldwide health crisis has turned 2020 into a year that no-one expected. A year that will certainly be remembered for a very long time. From stability to destabilisation. From normality to - ??? All we hear about on the news is about Corona virus. Nearly everything we hear when conversing with others is about Covid 19... Facebook, news, papers... This issue has given many people changes and challenges. There are significant mandatory rules in each country – isolated from family, from friends, and often workplaces... The situation has so many widespread impacts and ramifications. Some people say to "find the opportunities and positives", but for others this will be the challenge. Some will experience fear, anxiety and paranoia, while others will re-focus, re-engage and increase their resilience. Where will you be?

This chapter will consider the home environment. It is a Psychologists perspective on how to improve your wellbeing during this time. We will consider how you and your family can not only survive, but "thrive". This chapter will look at how you can move from feeling overwhelmed and stressed, to engaged and connected. We will examine some alternative ways of thinking and some strategies that will assist you at this time.

The Areas Covered Include:

- Family Interactions/Dynamics

- Self-Care

- Child Interactions

- Parent-Child Relationships

- Couple Relationships

Around the world, Psychologists are known for their skills and expertise. As mental health professionals, Psychologists can assist in a range of ways – this can include consulting with Government and organisations, to providing counselling or therapy. Some Psychologists are involved in creating policy or developing resources for the public. In these challenging times, many people access the internet for resources, support or information. As a Psychologist, I contribute in writing (blogs, book chapters, e-books), in presentations (at Conferences or to the general public), in training new Psychologists and in consulting directly with people (face to face or online/telehealth). **As A Psychologist My Passion Is All Aspects Of Wellbeing And Helping To Improve Life!**

The situation itself is a significant trigger for many people. A trigger of anxiety, fear and emotional disturbance. Some people in the community are worried, really worried about their own health, or about the health of their loved ones. This worry can be real or it can be escalating anxiety. For some people there is a fear, even a paranoia about the illness and what could happen. Some people are acting irrationally or being offensive in their interactions with others. These attitudes and behaviour leads to other actions and behaviours – some people are therefore "self-isolating" to protect themselves and their family, other people are "self-isolating" to protect community members who may be vulnerable. Each country around the world has a different rule or requirement at different times right now. What we need to remember is the importance of RESPECT in all of this. It is a challenging time but all of us have individual responsibility.

Family Interactions

Spending time together is great – right? There are so many things we can do. For some families, being together is fun and enjoyable. For other families, it is stressful, distressing, boring or even conflictual. For some people – the holidays are a "breeze", while for others it is a huge challenge. So when the country changes the rules – and there are people being isolated, and when things are cancelled and changed or don't happen. This is a big surprise, a challenge or even distressful.

We know that children gain comfort and security from routines as well as a range of things in their life. (Adults too can find that routines and regularity provide stability and consistency). For children, this can involve a positive relationship with their parents and a consistent routine. When parents understand their child (and their emotions) then the child is better able to be free to share their emotions.

The majority of people would be aware that stress impacts on our functioning, and on our immune system. It impacts on our sleep, our emotion management, and our interactions with others. So, spending time with others can be great, or it can be distressing. Everyone's tolerance is different, and interactions in our family and community impact on our mental health and daily functioning.

Being isolated can be a particular challenge. So also, can being stuck in a small space with the same people for a period of time. It will be important for parents and families to closely monitor their mood and interactions.

Parents are the role models for children. Children are watching – watching how their parents deal with emotions, or conflict, interactions with others or even themselves. So, as children grow, they learn to make choices and to experience responsibility and consequences. Parents are there to guide and assist children, and the strength of the parent- child relationship is most important. Have a think about how your parent-child relationship is going and what could be different.

A Few Strategies To Assist:

• Having some fun things to do together. Board games. Listening to music. Gardening.

• Having some time apart – doing what each of us are interested in. Reading a book, going to the park. Listening to music or drawing.

• Maintaining consistency with routines is important – eating, breaks, sleeping.

- Engaging with a counsellor or Psychologist to provide support for managing emotions or for parenting and relationship support. This can be face to face or telehealth. Many counsellors and Psychologists are providing online sessions at this time.

Is Home Schooling Driving You Nuts?

Suddenly found yourself stuck at home with the kids? All over our country, indeed, around the world – Schools maybe been shut down by the Government, and there are so many changes in our world. Staying home can be a challenge for many people – particularly if there are a few kids in the mix. Its sometimes a challenge when everyone is home on the holidays – but this is everyone home, for a much longer time AND to do school work. So you are all stuck at home together – everyday! So it's not unusual for parents to be feeling like they are "nuts" or "losing it" or that things can get out of control. You didn't train to be a "teacher", right? This could be even tougher than usual parenting. Change can be hard for everyone to deal with and we have some things that will help.

Managing Kids' Emotions

It can be a challenge for kids on a number of levels – change, emotions, siblings, home environment instead of school Now they've got mum or dad telling them what to do all day – that could be tough. Some kids manage their emotions well and others can be easily triggered into meltdown with changes, with no familiar school environment, with siblings nearby, with the struggles of a parent in a different role.

So Here Are A Few Tips To Help Your Kids:

1	Set out a clear visual structure with regular activity breaks.
2	Give kids a choice on what to do e.g. – would you like to do maths or spelling first.
3	Have time together to do some fun things – this will help with improving your relationship and connection.
4	Allow children some time to express emotions & energy (trampoline, kick a ball around).

Helping Parents To Cope:

Many parents are struggling with the changes too. If everyone is together in the same space for all day and every day, for days on end that can be tough. Ok – it might feel like you are "going nuts!" but you're not the only one - chances are, everyone else is feeling like that too.

Here Are Some Things To Help:

1	Get a good night's sleep (if that's hard, seek professional advice!).
2	Have some regular alone time (go for a walk in the garden or to the park).
3	Have someone you can debrief with (partner, friend, parent or professional).

Being home with your child – or all your kids can be challenging. Home schooling can be very different. There is a way to get through this and still enjoy life! You can survive! You will survive! Implement these family friendly strategies and find some things you can enjoy doing together – not only at the end of the day but during the day as well.

If things continue to be challenging – contact a Psychologist for a confidential consultation. We can provide parenting advice, information or counselling. You can receive counselling for parents or children – spending time with a professional can assist in better understanding your body and emotions.

Self-Care

Looking after yourself when "stuck at home" could be a challenge for many people. Some people live by themselves and like to be alone others may live by themselves and thrive on being social and interacting with a range of people. Others are by themselves but already have anxieties, depression or other mental health challenges to manage.

Some people live with a partner or family – but still, the challenges of self-care are relevant. Many people participate in team sports (can't do that now) or in catching up with friends (certainly not allowed in many countries). Some people find purpose and meaning in their work or in the community (volunteering or personal projects). All of this is now reduced or removed, which means that many people are now at home in the same space as all their family.

It's important first to be aware of how you are going. That involves some self-awareness and some self-reflection. Managing your emotions and managing your responses and your interactions with others. Many people find that physical activity can assist in their overall wellbeing, but also in their emotion management. Being able to spend some time in nature will greatly assist, but if you can't be outside, then listen to some relaxing music, maybe even some active music – and find some form of physical activity that will work for you. Some people like gym, others enjoy yoga, while others need to ride a bike, walk or swim.

Here's Some Things To Help:

1	Participate in physical activity.
2	Have a goal or a project to get involved in.
3	Listen to some music.
4	Do something that is relaxing for you (bath, cook, read a book, sit in the sun, garden).

Children & Child Interactions:

Each child is different and will experience things differently. A child who usually copes with life "fine" may still be "fine" or they may decline. As outlined earlier though, "change" can create another "change" and so as a parent "be aware" and "be alert" as things may be challenging for a while. It may be your child usually copes well with the routine and structure of life and now, things are different. It may be that your child is struggling with not playing with or seeing their friends. Maybe the home isolation is confronting, all that news on the virus and the people dying and their own anxiety has increased. Or perhaps, it's all your children just annoying each other, being in each other's personal space, and pushing the "buttons"!

Some Considerations For What May Assist:

1. Your child will need some alone time too…
2. Helping your child manage their emotions, reflecting their feelings, showing that you understand.
3. Physical activity is great for assisting with emotion management.
4. Check out some great websites.

Parent-Child Relationships:

Over the years, I have seen and heard many parents share their difficulties, concerns and challenges. The biggest concerns that parents have are often around children and their emotions. This often looks like tantrums, "losing it" and "meltdowns". Sometimes, this situation is related to other developmental challenges, sensory sensitivities or complex considerations like Autism. However, depending on their age, many children do actually have control over their emotions. It may just be that the situation has triggered them very fast into overwhelm or emotional overload.

Sometimes children have some low level anxiety – basically they are worried about something. Sometimes it is "change" and sometimes it is a situation that has occurred before – something that previously was stressful or distressing. For some children it is new things, or things that are out of their routine. For other children it is a situation where their brain is thinking, over thinking or needing many small, minor details resolved. This brain activity may cause their body to experience a range of emotions that are difficult to manage. Some children are not aware of their thought processes, just the feelings in their body. So everyone is different and experiences life differently.

The First Thing That Parents Can Do To Help Their Children With Behaviour, Is To Help Children With Their Feelings. This Can Happen In A Few Ways. Most Importantly, For The Parent To Acknowledge The Child's Feelings. For Example, "Johnny, I Can See That You Are Upset" Or "Mary, You Look Like That Is Frustrating You". This Helps A Child See That You Are Noticing Their Feelings, And Interested In Them. If Your Child Thinks You Go The "Feeling" That You Identified As "Wrong" Then I Am Sure That They Will Let You Know – And You Can Then Respond; "Oh, Ahh You Are Feeling

Annoyed - Not Angry". Again, This Helps The Child See That You Are Noticing Their Feelings And That They Are Being Focussed On.

A Second key strategy is to spend one on one time with your child. Many parents think that they have a good relationship with their child, but often don't realise that this relationship is often on specific terms and with a specific focus. Many parents and children benefit from having some "special time" together each week. For example, half an hour together – where the child decides the activity and the parent is responsive. For example, instead of the parent suggesting activity or playing the way that "they" want to then in this specific activity the child takes the lead and the parent is respectful of this and lets the child "lead". In some therapeutic techniques this is often referred to as "Special Time" within Filial Therapy or child-parent relationship therapy. A number of professionals are able to provide Parent skills training in techniques that assist the parent to be more responsive and attuned in their relationship.

Another strategy for helping children involves the parent having a consistent routine and clear boundaries. It's important for children to feel safe and secure and a regular routine will assist with that. It may be more challenging for children (if their parents are separated), for the child/children to have a routine across both care environments. But it can be done, particularly when parents are able to communicate respectfully together and to collaborate with their ex-partner. Many children have difficulty concentrating at school, or difficulty managing their emotions, simply because they are tired or overtired. It is important for everyone in the family to have a good nights' sleep.

It is important for children and their parents to respect and care for each other. Being able to communicate feelings is essential in any relationship.

Couple Relationships

Being in a relationship can have its challenges. There are many people who will be happy in their relationship, but this widespread change may even rock their boat. A change in one aspect of our life, can impact in other areas. Some couples maybe in a good routine, and this situation can change things for them. Maybe the time together balance is great, but now you have to be together all day, every day and that's tough. Maybe you need your space, your individual time. Maybe you each need social time and can't get it now. So many things that are now different.

Some couples will have challenges that are broader and far reaching. One partner or both may lose their job. This can add extra stress and difficulties. Perhaps one partner now needs to give up their job to be responsible for providing supervision or schooling for the child/children. This can create extra strain and additional challenges. For others, the changes can be more positive – allowing them time they don't usually have.

A forced "slow-down" can have some beneficial side effects – more time together, more relaxing and more togetherness.

Ultimately your partner needs you to care for them, and respect them. Allowing them to meet their individual needs will assist in the relational aspects. Taking it easy on each other – being more supportive and understanding in these challenging times.

A Few Things That Can Assist Include:

1. Having some time together separate to the children (maybe in means taking turns for "my time" and allowing your partner to rejuvenate or recuperate).
2. Arranging a date night – in-house- but something special!
3. Find out about "the 5 love languages" and do the quiz...

Your well-being during the corona virus is important. You are a part of a family, a community, a country, a world. Being connected is important. Engaging with your friends and family, in whatever ways are allowable and appropriate for where you are living right now. Make some conscious decisions to move from the stress and overwhelmed bubble – and head on over to the engaged and connected sphere.

There are many challenges and I hope that this information has been helpful.

By Jay Anderson

About the author

Jay is a Psychologist, Coach and Counsellor. She has over 25 year's experience in helping people with a range of challenges. Jay lives in southwest Western Australia - engaging with clients online and in person at the Southwest Wellbeing Centre. Jay's passion is "making a difference" and she is excited to be a part of this important project.

To find out more you will find Jay at:

Website: http://www.swwellbeing.com.au

If you would like to join our mailing list or receive a free e-book on Better understanding your well-being, then I can be contacted for more information on info@swwellbeing.com.au

Recommended Resources:

Gary Chapman-1992:

The Five Love Languages: How to Express Heartfelt Commitment to Your Mate

Gary Chapman and Ross Campbell 2016:

The Five Love Languages Of Children

Hand in Hand Parenting.org.

Stan Ferguson 2010:

What Parents Need To Know About Children

In Captivity And Isolation, We Found Freedom

The strange times we are in now are speculated to be because of many things... 5G Related, Biological war, and many other theories lie behind this global crisis we as human beings now find ourselves in. However it got here, we are all now very much in it and affected by it. Months in lock down, and the government have put us all under house arrest for the good of all, to protect the vulnerable. There is to be no school, no commute to work, no clubs, not even free for all at the shops, no nothing. Stay in your homes and in your gardens, with your family.

When historians tell of this time, which they will of course and the people read about our situation and our freedoms taken away, what will they think? I believe they will think, this was the beginning of the great awakening, this was the catalyst for change, this was the time in history when the human being remembered who they were and what they were; free from labels, student, manager, businessman or otherwise, when the human being realised that they had been living in captivity since the day they were born in to the system. They were born in to a nation of human doings not beings and the Earth allowed a virus to help them wake up and see, how little freedom they have and yet how much they can have, if they just take their personal power back.

You Have Been Given The Luxury Of Time

In captivity/isolation the people could breathe. They were present with the ones they love whether they lived together or apart, they become conscious. They planted food, they checked on strangers and neighbours they stopped polluting their world and their souls.

In our everyday lives we trade time with ourselves and our loved ones for money so we can buy food, pay for water and power and a roof over our head; but not just that, the latest phone, gadget, handbag etc. We have become a very excess oriented society. The society of not enough and I must have bigger and better has wreaked havoc in our relationships with ourselves and each other, the mental health of not just adults but children.

We have depleted our nature and nature around us on a catastrophic level. We have tipped the balance and it has not gone in the favour of our emotional, mental or physical wellbeing

This is our time now human beings. How can you stay sane and mentally healthy at this time of perceived lack of freedom? Put simply, remember who you are. Remember who you were before the world told you who you are and what you must do. Spiritual beings having a human experience with more power than you can imagine as an individual and collectively.

Right now, is our opportunity for spiritual and personal growth and rest and repair. Yes there is much uncertainty for many of us and for the world, but we are more than a number in our bank as much as we are more than a number on the scales and for the first time the system has been forced in to closure, giving us time to wake up and be the change we want to see in our personal lives and in our collective consciousness.

So, what can we do? Well firstly let us get over the guilt at doing nothing, this is all part of the human doing sickness we are so heavily indoctrinated in. Just do nothing, be nothing but you and then begin to start the very overdue conversation with yourself.

The sheer magnitude of all that is happening is overwhelming, all change starts from one act and a ripple effect that follows, that is how the Corona virus exists and that is how any virus or trouble begins is with one action. It is also the same for the good things that come, it all comes from one action, the good comes from the human spirit being strong in its power to create change, stand up for what is right and true and right now the focus is on YOU, YOU are superhero of this story. It is time to ask yourself some questions that can, if you wish change your life.

Being able to bring about change first requires the time to acknowledge that you need or want it. This is the gift in the crisis. A time of reflection before the human doing machine finds the reboot button and wants you to go back to business as usual against your souls yearning.

We only have one thing we must do on this planet and that is to be who we truly are, which is love. WE must be and do love in every word and action, this is our place of indestructible power.

When we are who we want to be and we do what our soul intended us to do, our heart is happy our stress levels reduced. We are at peace with ourselves as we are not resisting our true essence, the essence of who we are paves the way for our own wonderful life, which in turn touches others and inspires and motivates them to do the same.

Use this precious gift of time to ask yourself reflective questions. Spend time alone at night or day depending on your household and its noise levels. (I am a mum of 6 so I grab before they get up or in the middle of the night). In the quiet, in the stillness, breathe deep, and have this intimate conversation with yourself. The only real conversation that matters is the one no one teaches us to have until we have traded so much of our essence, so much of our time and happiness that we are too far down the rabbit hole to notice that we have just been coasting in someone else's story, too powerless and distracted to step in to our own.

Intimate conversations require an intimate setting, so if you are not sure how to hear your hearts voice in your head, I suggest you set the stage. To get the best results you must limit to eliminate toxins.

Imagine you are preparing for one of the most important conversations of your life, be it career or relationship related, you wouldn't go in intoxicated and unprepared you would be ready, clear head, on a mission to pursue or accept big changes, strong of body and mind, calm and collected.

Suggested Actions To Take:

- Avoid Caffeine – It is an unnecessary stimulant that goes against being calm and open, interrupts natural sleep patterns and can cause you to feel anxious, taking you out of the relaxed rest and repair state that we need to stay in for our task.
- Choose herbal teas, hot lemon water - Any drink that hydrates the cells of the body rather than ask it to do extra work.
- Don't eat a huge stodgy meal or big take away then go and try and create this conversation. You could feel physically fatigued and potentially have a sluggish negative mind-set.
- Avoid Sugar – The sugar blues is a real thing, when we want to connect with our highest self, we need to leave the self-sabotaging, toxic, stimulating factors at the door.
- Eat a diet high in plant-based foods. All food has a vibration; natural, organic plant-based foods provide our body and mind the highest vibrational fuel for the healthiest body and mind. The more open and calm the body is the more receptive the heart mind connection and the clearer the communication.

- Include Superfoods. Superfoods are always good, named that way as they provide you so much, it is a subject matter in itself but when your body receives nutrient dense, high vibrational foods your stress levels are reduced, your happiness comes easier and your immune system stays strong in defence. I currently would recommend a spoonful of spirulina a day in some fresh orange juice or a well-balanced smoothie. Its ability to heighten you on both physical and spiritual level is never more so important as it is now.
- Spend time in the fresh air, this may be from your balcony, window, garden or a local quiet walk anywhere you are isolated for the reasons of the global pandemic but also so you can make space for your spirit to talk to you and so you have to time to reflect on all you have to be grateful for in the world of never ending abundance.

The above recommendations are not essential for the conversation with self but will help you get the best results; a polluted body is a polluted mind so, a well-nourished and nurtured body will give you a clear, healthy mind.

Set The Stage By Creating A Mini Ritual:

Essential Tools:

Pen and Journal - For me, my journal is a conversation with myself and makes sense and silence out of the mental madness my mind likes to try and inflict on me.

Optional Extras And Highly Recommend:

Essential oils or incense:

A great one for meditation is frankincense. It is of course the king of oils and hey it if is good enough for Jesus it is good enough for us, right? Frankincense is so high vibrational; it literally raises your cellular health. This means it is great for immunity as well as fighting depression it calms the mind soothe our fears, and works on the pineal gland which is what the ancients documented as being the window, not just to our soul but to the universe itself.

You may need some meditation music or just your favourite tunes that help ground you and any racing thoughts. Breathing deeply, slowly relaxes your whole body, making it easier to connect with

your mind, heart and soul. I personally like the alternate nostril breathing, there are many advantageous ways to breathe to relax body and mind and I encourage you to find the one that works best for you. The only important 'MUST DO' about this conversation is having it openly and honestly and making it happen.

Start This Very Important Conversation With The Suggested Following Questions:

Q. How do you normally spend your time? Does it make you happy? If not, why? How would you like to spend your time? Can you do that now, or can you see how you can make it possible?

Q. What value do I add to the lives of others?

Q. Do I practice self-care? Do I look after myself like I do those I love? If not, how can you start doing this?

Q. How reliant am I on a system to provide for my basic needs of food and hydration? Can I become more self-sufficient? What steps can I take to be able to provide for my basic needs and that of those I love?

Q. What are you passionate about? Have you forgotten what you're passionate about? Do you do or have what you are passionate about? If now how can you change this?

Q What would happen if I do not be who I am and pursue things I truly love? What will my life legacy be?

Q. Am I kind? Am I caring?

Q. Do you value your physical body, which is the vehicle for your soul's life purpose, or do you find you ask too much of it and need to give back.

Q. Do you like what you see? Are you happy? Is there anything you wish was different?

There is no limit to the questions you can ask, it is your conversation. These are helpful suggestions to use this crisis as a gift to *'know thyself'*. Know that you are important, you are worthy of all the happiness you crave and deserve. Nothing is too big a leap if it is your hearts calling, help yourself and help your fellow human and together in our awakened consciousness we can help give back to the earth that we have ravaged so fiercely over the past 60 years.

Remember we are all as one, all part of the cosmos, all crucial and essential. We matter, what we do or do not do matters. Chose this gift of time to remember who you are and be that human. Life and the world we are part of is more wonderful than you have been able to see. Now is your time, now is our time, the time of the rise of the Human being and the fall of the human doing and the powers that enforce this outdated system of take more than you give.

WAKE UP, YOU HAVE TIME, BE THE CHANGE,

WE ARE ONE, WE ARE LOVE, ONLY LOVE IS REAL

Knowing yourself is the beginning of all wisdom - Aristotle

Rebecca McQueen

About the author

I am a proud mother to 6 wonderful children and a health coach who has 10 professional years helping people with both their physical and emotional well-being.

I suffered with anxiety and depression from a very young age which was the driving force behind my passion for self-discovery and wellness.

Years later I made my passion and purpose my profession and have had the privilege of helping others rediscover who they are, align with their purpose and look after their body and mind.

I love what I do, I love people, the planet and the journey.

https://www.stresslesshealthcoach.co.uk/

How To Stay Creative And Keep Your Family Sane During Lockdown

Lockdown came, and all of a sudden, me and my wife were not just parents to our 4 children (2 boys aged 11 and 8 and a boy and a girl twins ages 2) – we were teachers, exercise coaches, 'pseudo' school friends and chefs. Being holed up at home with your loved ones can put strain on relationships, especially when concern about the current circumstances already has sentiments running high.

Ordinarily, there is grandma and grandpa, for extended family caregiving. But with the elderly especially at risk, we found ourselves on our own. But there are things we can all do to help us get along with our families better, by maintaining strong relationships and avoiding clashes and frustrations during this unprecedented time in our lives.

Establish A Routine

From the onset of Lockdown, the schools were setting the older children work on their platforms. Supervising, our children's learning from home, while running a business from home was initially a struggle. The stay-at-home orders left us stressed without routines, but we quickly found that creating a schedule for our family was a way to regain, even in a small way, a sense of order and regularity. Whatever your daily routine looks like, the certainty and consistency of this structure can bring comfort to you and your family during these indeterminate times.

We maintain as much 'normal' as we can by establishing daily routines for things like defined morning routines, meal times, exercise times, a specific end point to the school day or working day and a calming bedtime. We have discovered that it is important to try to delineate week-ends as different. Although, this mainly applies to my older children.

During the day we try to eliminate screen distractions as much as possible. However, we appreciate the importance for the older children to connect with their peers and teachers so that they do not feel isolated. In order to break the day up we create a list one day in advance with 3 different breaks activities that the older children can pick for the following day, and give them 10 minutes to enjoy that break-time activity.

Needless to say, that there isn't a one-size-fits-all way to schedule every child. Our eldest son finds security in following a school-like timetable, whereas our middle son thrives on a more child-led, free-flowing approach, but all of our children need some predictability in their lives. At the end of each day we set aside time to talk about how our day went, face time extended family members, play a board games, read, or walk the dog.

Limit Exposure To The Media

In my opinion as the media tries to understand the scope of this unprecedented, global health crisis, its coverage of the coronavirus pandemic has been raucous, to say the least. And once shared among friends, the quantity of constantly-changing news updates can be disconcerting. For this reason, I limit myself to only browsing official websites rather than Instagram or Facebook feeds for my daily updates on the pandemic.

We try to keep talk about the Corona Virus to a minimum around the house. Understandably, the older children have lots questions and we answer them honestly, factually and age-appropriately – but we try not to focus all of our family conversations on the Covid 19.

Embrace Family Time

Being so accessible to each other every day can make it easy to forget to find quality family time and focus on emotional connections. Against the sad backdrop of the coronavirus, we are rediscovering the pleasure of spending time with each other and our children. Lockdown has been an opportunity to nurture our relationships and enjoy each other's company with fun activities and games such as:

- ***Zoom*** – just because the children might not be able to physically be with their grandparents, doesn't mean they can't see them.
- ***Movie Nights*** – it's the perfect opportunity to bond with all members of the family - and the children cherish curling up with us and each other on the couch and sharing in the experience playing out on the screen. It's the stuff childhood memories are made of.
- Making Obstacle Courses – as part of our Easter Egg hunt me and my wife created an obstacle course using objects from around the house like boxes, a skipping rope and hula-hoops, and an egg and spoon.
- Board Dames – from now on Friday nights in the Dattani household will be for games. It's been the perfect way to teach the children about teamwork, patience, and how to win and lose gracefully.
- ***Jigsaw Puzzles*** – we've being doing puzzles every day with the twins. Initially we started off with 4-piece puzzles and through lockdown

- have progressed to 16-piece puzzles. Ultimately, the most important thing is the fun involved in playing with puzzles! The twins enjoy learning the most when they are having fun.
- **Reading Together** – in the evening we have family reading time, where me and my wife read to the twins and the older children get to read a book of their choice. Cuddling up with a storybook at bedtime provides routine and stability, essential for children as they learn best through gentle repetition.
- **Arts And Crafts** - instead of buying bubbles from the shop, we make it into an arts and crafts project. The older children made bubble solution warm water and washing up liquid and made DIY bubble wands using pipe cleaners. The twins and dog spend entire afternoons running around catching them.
- **Gardening** - planting is not only fun, but also long-term activity, it's been nice for us to watch the plants the children have planted grow and take part in nurturing and caring for them.
- Spotting wildlife – this has been a favourite with the older children. Since moving to Stanmore in 2016, we'd seen grey squirrels, wood pigeons, magpies, crows and and gulls but had never seen hedgehogs, muntjac deer, foxes, green woodpeckers, pied wagtails, red kites, grass snakes, ringneck parakeets, mute swans, robins, Canada geese, Pipistrelle Bats, great tits, wrens, finches, herons, toads an egret and many other species of birds and insects that we haven't yet been able to identify. All within 5 minutes' walk of our house!
- Picnics and BBQ's - Whenever the sun is out, we take a blanket and BBQ outside, some healthy foods to make sure we get our daily dose of vitamin D.
- Housework – lockdown has been the perfect time to teach the older children to learn what it takes to run a household. We've devised a rota where they each have specific jobs they need to do, like putting away the dishes, hoovering or helping hang up clothes.

Exercise

When compared to the spectre of death and global economic collapse, having to take time off from exercising seems pretty low on the list of calamities caused by the lockdown, but exercise is especially important now, even when the logistics are more challenging because it boosts us physically and mentally.

As well as the physical health benefits, keeping active is a great way to ward off some of the psychological issues associated with being cooped up for an extended time.

I start my mornings with a brisk 30-minute dog walk. He is naturally in the present, so watching him run around helps me think the same, and it puts a smile on my face. It also forces me to go outside, when I might otherwise sit inside on a cold day. When back at home I do some stretching and breathing exercises.

During the week, we all do a Joe Wicks home workout, although aimed at children the whole family gets involved.

I've found that the simplest way to work out at home is to use your own body weight, and for good reason. Push ups and squats are fundamental pieces of any fitness routine, and you need to hold mastery over them.

They can help you build strength, endurance and burn calories. And by circuit training (going from one exercise to the next, without little or no rest), you keep your heart rate up, burn more calories and get the most out of your exercise time.

Body-weight HIIT workouts are relatively short and don't take up much space. Best of all, they don't require any equipment.

Although as a family we've always eaten relatively healthily, since lockdown we have eaten healthier than we normally would. When in the office I usually buy a meal deal or grab sandwich for lunch every day.

At home we put a lot of effort into all of our meals. We always use fresh fruit and veg, season it, take no shortcuts with low-nutrition frozen stuff, and avoid grazing all day on junk food.

Patience and Understanding

At a time when we all face uncertainty and worry about coronavirus, such changes in our relationships are all the harder to cope with. So, it is worth trying to be extra patient and understanding, both with each other and also ourselves.

Being in each other's pockets at all times is bound to aggravate any strain you might be feeling. In the Dattani household, we have designated different areas to different family members and/or uses (e.g. work, play, homework) to ensure we all have the space (and privacy) to complete tasks without interruption.

It is also important to encourage time out and space for everyone so they can unwind and have some time alone.

We try to work out a set of boundaries with the children so they understand our expectations and we can grasp theirs too. We build in family time in the day so the children feel supported. Ensuring that they have structure through their day minimises any potential conflict.

The lockdown has meant a different rhythm of life, a chance to be in touch with others in different ways than usual.

To conclude, it helps to try and see this time as a different period of time in your life, and not necessarily a bad one, even if you didn't choose it. Our new daily routine prioritises looking after ourselves. As a family we read more, watch more movies, have a daily exercise routine and have tried new relaxation techniques. The lockdown has taught us that whenever people are forced to collectively and radically change their daily lives, due to an external event, its brings a shared joint experience that we will continue to talk about in the years to come; a sense of having all been "in it together." We hold onto that feeling. We remind each other that it is in the very near future.

The older children have started keeping a daily diary. It is a great way for them to keep track of quarantine life, record memories and note down aspirations and emotions. For us the best thing to have come out of lockdown is that as a family we are letting the outdoors recharge us. As nature heals, so do we. We've been forced to pause, slow down, reflect and appreciate the little things our front and back gardens, local woodland and lake have to offer – from morning birdsongs to the riot of pastel colours pouring from our seasonal blossom trees.

Thanks to quarantine, we have found that there's something beautiful about reconnecting with the great outdoors, whether that's through gardening and nature spotting on outdoor walks.

Ketan Dattani

About the author

Ketan Dattani is the Founding Owner and CEO of Buckingham Futures, a specialist award winning Environmental Recruitment Business that provides bespoke permanent and temporary recruitment and consultancy solutions to public and private sector employers.

He has a high profile within the Recruitment sector and is widely recognised as an expert on Employment Law, Employee rights, CV writing and for providing Careers Advice.

Academically he is a graduate of Environmental Biology and a post graduate of Environmental Planning and Management.

He also holds a Certificate in Employment Law and The Certificate in Recruitment Practice which is a nationally recognised recruitment qualification developed jointly by the REC and key employers.

He began his career in recruitment in 1998 and in 2013 Ketan set up Buckingham Futures.

Foods to Boost the Immune System

Love Your Immune System

Are you curious to find out how changing what you eat might help your immune system? Up until now, you probably haven't given your immune system much thought – yet it's been quietly keeping you safe since you were born!

Your immune system is your best friend. During the Corona-virus pandemic, more than ever, you need your best friend, to keep you safe. Best friends - are friends for life – quite literally!

Just like any friendship, you need to treat each other with respect. Treat your immune system with love and kindness, and it will reward you by warding off horrible infections, cancer and heart disease too. Mistreat your immune system and it will let you down, sometimes with serious consequences.

- What's the best way to look after your immune system?
- How is your immune response affected by what you eat?
- What are the best foods you can eat to support your immune system?

I sincerely hope you will understand that this chapter is not just a long list of healthy foods. To improve your immune system, you need to eat to live – not live to eat. If you can understand the connection between what you put in your mouth, and how this affects all aspects of your health including your immune system, this will help motivate you to make major positive dietary changes for the long term.

Only 5% of Americans are estimated to currently be at their correct weight due to a healthy combination of eating the right foods and taking the right amount of physical exercise. That's a staggering thought! So, this chapter is for the 95% of you who really need to make some serious changes.

So ... let's get started.

What Is The Immune System?

Let's begin with a brief, overview of the immune system. We can only marvel at the infinite numbers of complex, inter-related, and sophisticated, biochemical reactions taking place in our bodies - a gigantic, microbiological fairground - making us what we are today.

The Immune System

The immune system is a highly complex network of specialised white blood cells - lymphocytes, neutrophils, monocytes, and macrophages - which are constantly circulating in your bloodstream. These cells travel inside lymphatic channels, which run alongside your blood vessels. Lymphocytes are stored at various sites in your body, for example, in your lymph nodes, and also in your spleen. They are called to action when a defence is required.

Function Of The Immune System

Your body is constantly under attack from the outside world. Any cell it does not recognise as one of your own is a potential threat and needs to be destroyed. These foreign invaders include bacteria, viruses, protozoa and fungi. However, any of your own cells which have been damaged, and are not fit for purpose, are also killed and removed in the same way. These cells may be early cancer cells. Your body is working tirelessly, 24/7, to protect you and keep you well.

T Cells And B Cells

There are three types of lymphocytes – T lymphocytes, B lymphocytes and Natural Killer (NK) Cells. They pass messages to each other via the release of specific molecules which act as chemical messengers. The immune response involves highly sophisticated, cell-signaling pathways.

T Lymphocytes – known as T cells, are involved in cell-mediated immunity. This is an immune response which does not involve antibodies. Once a cell is identified as foreign, special proteins called cytokines, are released. Important cytokines include interleukins, interferons and tumour necrosis factor (TNF-alpha). The release of cytokines signals the arrival of macrophages, cells which physically - 'eat up!' - the foreign cell - and destroy it.

B- Lymphocytes – known as B-cells, are involved in producing an antibody response. All cells carry shapes on their surface called antigens. Your body learns which are yours and which are not and remembers this. As soon as your body recognises a foreign antigen, it produces an antibody, which sticks to the foreign antigen, and neutralises the attack. Anti-bodies are immunoglobulins, special proteins - made-to-measure for the job.

When The Immune Response Is Switched On – This Causes Inflammation:

Acute Inflammation – this occurs, for example, when a streptococcal bacterium settles on your tonsil. The tonsils are red, swollen, and painful and you have a fever.

Chronic Inflammation occurs, for example, when you develop an on-going problem such as osteoarthritis in your knee. The knee continues to be red, hot, swollen and painful.

Chronic inflammation, however, has negative health consequences for your body. Read more about this further on.

What Does The Immune System Need To Function?

For your immune system to function correctly, all the components need to be fully functioning and in good working order. These biochemical processes require essential macronutrients e.g. fats, proteins, carbohydrates, and micronutrients e.g. vitamins and minerals.

Your body is just one great big machine. Like a car which needs petrol, oil and new spark plugs, your body needs the correct food, water, and nourishment. How do we know this? Let's look at this from the opposite angle - malnutrition greatly increases your susceptibility to disease.

Malnutrition Doesn't Only Affect Third World Countries – It Also Affects The Western World

Malnutrition is a major recognised cause of immunodeficiency. Sadly, in third world countries, extreme lack of food results in weight loss. There is a general break-down of gut-barrier function, making it easier for pathogens to pass through the gut wall into the body. Weakness, loss of appetite and dehydration further compound the problem. Overall, this results in a weakened immune system. More than half of children under age 5 die because of increased susceptibility to infections such as measles, malaria and HIV.

However, the problem is not unique to the third world. Even in civilised countries, much of the population is undernourished. In the USA, 15% of the ambulant populations are malnourished, as are 25-60% of patients in long term care and 35-65% of those in hospital.

In the USA, 37 million adults are hungry, including 11 million children, according to the website Feeding America.

Even those who are eating, are living on fast and processed foods, and many have no idea of the dangers. In his fascinating 2018 paper in the *Journal of Lifestyle Medicine*, Dr Joel Fuhrman describes the dietary habits of Americans as 'fast-food genocide.' 71% of Americans are now obese – that's 100 million people.

Today, eating processed and fast foods is widely believed to kill more people than smoking.

Many people don't understand the link between poor diet and obesity, and how the direct effect of this affects the immune system, and ultimately increases their risk of heart disease, stroke, diabetes, cancer and dementia.

Please keep reading.

How To Boost Your Immune System Through Diet

Let's get something straight – boosting your immune system is not as simple as grabbing the odd apple, or taking a vitamin tablet every day. If you simply do this - but change nothing else about your health and habits - this is highly unlikely to produce any significant benefit. To help your immune system, you need to under-stand the concept of chronic inflammation.

What Is Chronic Inflammation?

Remember the description at the beginning of this chapter about how your immune system works and what it does in your body? Once the immune response is switched on, it starts the process of inflammation. And although this keeps us alive in the face of infection, a chronic inflammatory response in the body is dangerous for overall health. Chronic inflammation is the key underlying mechanism resulting in premature death from cardiovascular disease (heart attacks and strokes), diabetes, cancer and dementia. In chronic inflammation, the release of inflammatory cells causes atherosclerosis - the build-up of fatty plaques which eventually block the arteries, for example, causing a heart attack. These inflammatory cells also inadvertently cause cancer by failing to recognise and destroy other cells - damaged during every day wear and tear - but are now left behind to become early cancer cells. Inflammatory cells interfere with carbohydrate and fat metabolism leading to diabetes and exacerbating weight gain.

Bad News - Chronic inflammation is a silent killer and unchecked, it has a significant effect on your immune function. It's happening inside our bodies, but none of us realises what's going on.

Obesity is a direct cause of chronic inflammation. This is because hormones produced in adipose tissue set off the inflammatory cascade. Rates of obesity are at epidemic levels.

Here Are Two Key Messages -

- To reduce chronic inflammation, you need to lose weight.
- Weight loss is the most important tool available to boost your immune system.

Good news! - However, this does not mean starvation or working yourself to death in an expensive gym. You can do this by simply changing your diet to eat healthy nutritious food and increasing physical exercise as part of your daily routine. You just need motivation and determination!

You really can switch off the production of inflammatory markers and cytokines, which are damaging your tissues every day by making significant changes to your diet. This will also result in losing weight.

Antioxidants

Have you heard of antioxidants? These are clever molecules which 'switch off' chronic inflammation. They are found in many foods but notably in fruit and vegetables. To increase your intake of antioxidants, all you need is to eat a regular, balanced diet, containing an abundance of antioxidant-rich foods. Can't I just take an antioxidant tablet? I'm afraid that studies looking at the longer-term effects of taking antioxidant supplements have failed to show a significant benefit in humans. This is something which continues to puzzle scientists. You are strongly recommended to increase your antioxidant intake by making improvements to your diet.

How To Reduce Chronic Inflammation

There are other ways to reduce chronic inflammation. Measures such as stopping smoking, reducing alcohol consumption, increasing the amount of physical exercise, and getting enough sleep are also very important. However, in this chapter, the focus is on changing your diet.

A Healthy Diet

Eating the wrong foods has a dramatic effect on your health. What are the right foods? What should you be eating? Whichever diet you choose to follow, medical evidence suggests -

- **Reduce Red Meat** - especially processed meat e.g. salami, ham, sausages, bacon, and pre-cooked meats.
- **Adopt A Plant-Based Diet**. You do not necessarily have to become vegetarian or vegan but try to increase the quantity of plants and vegetables in your diet.
- **Reduce Your Intake Of Refined Carbohydrates** e.g. white flour, bread, pasta, pizza dough, and puddings. Very low carbohydrate diets (VLCD's) have proved very successful especially for diabetics or those with pre-diabetes. Limiting glucose consumption leads to fat breakdown.
- **Reduce Your Intake Of Saturated Fats** e.g. butter, cream, cheese, meat, chocolate, biscuits and pastries. Swap to unsaturated fats instead e.g. olive oil, rapeseed oil, avocado, almonds, walnuts, peanuts and oily fish.
- **Restrict Calorie Intake** - Calorie restriction has numerous health benefits. For example, in one 2015 study, those who restricted their

daily calorie consumption by 12% for 2 years had a 10% reduction in body weight and significant health improvements.

- **Eat More Foods With A Low Glycaemic Index** - The glycaemic index is a measure of how quickly sugar is released from food after eating. Foods with a high glycaemic index are sugary foods and drinks, white bread, white rice and pasta. These give a rapid spike in glucose levels and as they fall, you feel hungry again. Low glycaemic foods release sugar slowly so you feel fuller for longer. Low glycaemic foods include many fruits and vegetables, wholemeal grains, pulses and oats.

- **Increase Your Intake Of Dietary Fibre** - Fibre is very important as it bulks out the stool, improving intestinal transport. It also helps you feel full and lowers cholesterol. Fibre is found in whole grains, fruit and vegetables, potatoes in their jackets, and oats, for example,

- **Reduce The Amount Of Salt In Your Diet** –2.5 million deaths a year could be prevented around the world by cutting the amount of salt in the diet to the recommended level (WHO). Salt is found in processed foods e.g. bacon, salami, soy sauce, salty snacks, instant noodles and stock cubes.

- **Consider Going Longer Without Eating** - Fasting – There has been much interest in the effects of fasting on weight loss and health. After 8 hours of not eating, your liver has used up its stores of glucose and your body starts to break down fat. This is the basis of the 5:2 and the 16:8 diets.

What Is The Healthiest Diet?

The jury is still out on which diet is best to lose weight, keep it off, and maintain optimal health.

However, the principles are 2-fold:

- **Restrict calorie intake**
- **Increase physical exercise**

Your diet needs to be interesting, varied and satisfying, to enable you to stick to it long-term. This will differ according to personal taste and preference. One popular diet which ticks all these boxes is **The Mediterranean Diet**:

The principles of the Mediterranean Diet are very similar to the current American dietary guidelines issued by the USDA:

https://health.gov/sites/default/files/2019-09/2015-2020_Dietary_Guidelines.pdf Focus on high-quality foods and smaller portions.

Take a look at **The Healthy Plate:**

https://www.hsph.harvard.edu/nutritionsource/healthy-eating-plate/. Half of your plate should be made up of fruit and vegetables. One-quarter of your plate should be protein. The other quarter should consist of whole grains.

The Mediterranean Diet

The Mediterranean Diet has been the traditional diet of people who for generations, have lived around the Mediterranean Sea. The diet contains a large amount of fruit and vegetables, nuts, seeds and whole grains, with small amounts of lean meat, plus chicken and fish, and unsaturated fats such as olive oil. The Mediterranean Diet has is regarded as 'the gold standard' in preventive medicine, to quote a 2016 discussion paper in the Journal, *Current Opinion in Clinical Nutrition and Metabolic Care*. There is now a huge amount of evidence supporting the health benefits of this diet.

It is associated with lower risks of cardiovascular disease (strokes and heart attacks), heart failure, death and disability. This is because the diet is complete in terms of micronutrients and rich in antioxidants and which have potent anti-inflammatory properties.

The *Journal of Public Health and Nutrition* published a 2014 meta-analysis of prospective studies including over 4 million people, looking at the health benefits of the Mediterranean Diet. The authors concluded that for every 2 point score of adherence to the diet, there was an 8% reduction in all-cause mortality, a 10% reduction in death from cardiovascular disease and a 4% reduction is cancer.

https://pubmed.ncbi.nlm.nih.gov/24476641/?dopt=Abstract

A 2017 study in the *Journal of Nutrition* concluded that the Mediterranean Diet was associated with a 13% reduction in the development of type 2 diabetes.

The authors found that people following a diet high in 'unhealthy foods' e.g. red meat, processed foods, refined sugars and fat, were 44% more likely to develop type 2 diabetes. This compared to those eating a 'healthy foods,' e.g. white meat, fish, vegetables, fruits and whole grains, who reduced their risk of developing type-2 diabetes by 16%.

For more information - The Mediterranean Diet:

What is the Mediterranean Diet?   (https://www.nhs.uk/)

Plant-Based Diets

Plant-based diets are increasing in popularity. In the USA, according to one American Consumer Report, between 2014 - 2017 the numbers of vegans increased from 1% to 6%. In the UK, the Vegan Society website states that numbers have quadrupled between 2014 and 2019, with just over 1% of the population now vegan. Plant-based diets appear to offer significant health benefits. Adherence to the diet reduces obesity-related metabolic syndrome and leads to a reduction in chronic inflammation.

For example, in 2017, a paper in the journal *Nutrients* reviewed all the good quality, medical literature, published between 1980 - 2016. Being vegetarian reduced the risk of diabetes by around 30%

Advantages Of A Plant-Based Diet

- Plant-based foods have anti-inflammatory effects. For example, carotenoids and flavonoids found in fruit and vegetables are powerful antioxidants. Carotenoids are found in fruit and vegetables with bright orange or yellow pigments such as carrots, squash, and yellow peppers. Flavonoids are found in onions, broccoli, kale, berries, grapes, tea and lettuce.
- Eating a plant-based diet means you are not eating any meat. The 2018 American Institute for Cancer Research report warns that

cooking red meat leads to the production of heterocyclic amines and polycyclic hydrocarbons which have been linked to the development of colorectal cancer. High levels of haem iron in meat can also stimulate the development of cancer cells.

- The plant-based diet includes high levels of phytochemicals, which includes Vitamin C, for example – a powerful antioxidant, and a vital co-factor for many of the pathways involved in the immune response.

Vegan Diet Or Vegetarian Diet?

It's been impossible to say, hand over heart, that the vegan diet is the most beneficial. The vegan diet results in a lower intake of saturated fatty acids, which is good for health, and in addition, an increased intake of fibre, magnesium, iron, ferritin, vitamin B1, C and E. However, vegans have a lower intake of essential vitamins such as B12, D, calcium, zinc and protein.

Benefits Of Increasing Dietary Fibre - A huge 2019 review, looking at 135 million years of personal data, concluded that increasing fibre intake to the greatest intake of 25-29 g per day, resulted in a 15-30% reduction in death from all causes – including heart disease, type 3 diabetes and bowel cancer.

Lower Levels Of Vitamin B12 – However, 50% of vegans have been found to have low levels of vitamin B12 which can have serious health consequences.

Low B12 levels are associated with elevated homocysteine levels, and these are a marker for increased atherosclerosis, the major cause of coronary heart disease. Low B12 levels are also linked to stroke, Alzheimer's and Parkinson's Disease.

Anaemia - Iron deficient anaemia is also more common in vegans and vegetarian. This causes extreme fatigue, and if it becomes severe, can affect your heart function, for example. Anaemia is a serious medical condition.

The Verdict? - Vegans are recommended to consult their doctors while on a vegan diet and have regular blood tests and vitamin supplements.

What Is A Healthy Diet?

Macronutrients - To be nutritionally complete, you need to eat the correct amount, and the right type, of protein, fat, and carbohydrate, every day – see *Table 1: Healthy Diet Essentials*.

Micronutrients - Your diet must also contain the correct vitamin and mineral content.

Water-soluble vitamins are those which you absorb from your diet and any excess is excreted. These are vitamins B-1, B-2, B-3, B-5, B-6, B-7, B-9, and B-12, and vitamin C.

Fat-soluble vitamins are stored body fat and in your liver. These are vitamins A, D, E, and K. Your body makes Vitamin D in the skin in sunlight, but all other vitamins must come from the diet.

What's The Right Amount?

Rather than being too concerned about the amount of vitamins in foods, it's preferable to follow a varied diet containing a variety of fresh foods, fruit and vegetables.

There should be no need for taking vitamin supplements. Minerals are trace elements which derive from volcanic rock and soil. They form part of your diet when you eat animal produce or a plant food source which has grown outdoors. Essential minerals include calcium, chloride (salt), magnesium, potassium, sodium, chromium, copper, fluoride, iodine, iron, manganese, selenium, and zinc.

For more information - see the Harvard Medical School website:

https://www.health.harvard.edu/staying-healthy/the-best-foods-for-vitamins-and-minerals

If you adopt a healthy diet, for example, The Mediterranean Diet, this contains the correct balance of nutrition, and you can follow the diet easily, knowing your body is getting what it needs. Fad diets are often just that –

short term gimmicks which are not sustainable over the longer term and do not often health advantages. Your diet should be varied, interesting and make you feel full after eating. If you eat correctly and take some regular exercise, you will find you feel well and are not hungry.

If you need to snack choose fruit or vegetables, not high fat, high sugar snacks which give you a sugar rush and only make you crave more.

Table 1: Healthy Diet Essentials

	Protein	Fat	Carbohydrate
Adult average daily recommended intake Based on an average of 2000 calories per day	Male 88g Female 64g	No more than 35% daily calorie content from fat. Consume - **less saturated fat*** and	50% daily calorie content should be from carbohydrates – an average 225 - 330 g/day.
Main sources	Meat Fish Eggs Milk Cheese Cereal Cereal products Nuts Pulses Beans Lentils	**more unsaturated**** i.e. monounsaturated and polyunsaturated fats. *Saturated fat e.g. fatty meat, processed foods, butter, cakes, biscuits **Unsaturated fats e.g. olive oil, avocado, fatty fish, almonds, cashews, sesame seeds	Consume **more natural unrefined sugars,*** less **refined sugars.**** *Natural sugars e.g. in fruit and vegetables **Refined sugars e.g. table sugar, honey **Starch** e.g. bread, potatoes, pasta and rice. **Fibre** e.g. potatoes with their skins intact, fruits, nuts and vegetables
One adult portion size	100g lean meat, (red and poultry) 140g fish 2 medium eggs 3 tablespoons seeds/nuts	Look at food labels: <3g/100g total fat - low fat <1.5g/100g saturated fat – low in saturated fat	Examples: 1 medium baked potato 1 slice wholemeal bread 2-3 tablespoons rice 2-3 tablespoons pasta
Dietary tip	In any diet maintain the daily intake of protein	Use spray oils, such as olive oil, or measure with a teaspoon when cooking	Choose foods with a low glycaemic index e.g. whole grains, brown rice and pasta, porridge and pulses.

Table 1 – Data from the British Nutrition Society

https://www.nutrition.org.uk/

Superfoods – Why Bother?

Who's heard of superfoods? These are a top priority for healthy eating – here's why.

Although there is no agreed definition of superfoods, these foods have a high nutritional content and offer nutritional advantages over other foods. Many superfoods are fruit or vegetables and are frequently brightly coloured due to their rich natural pigments. In truth, the term 'superfoods' is controversial, as proven research of their health benefits in humans is lacking, however, many nutritionists remain convinced of their dietary advantages. Harvard Medical School advises that no single food can provide all the nutrition one person needs. Food should be eaten from all different good groups. They recommend that healthy dietary eating patterns can reduce the risk of high blood pressure, diabetes and cancer. The medical school specifically endorses the Mediterranean Diet. They stress the importance of including superfoods in your diet saying: "**Superfoods should be singled out for special recognition as they offer important nutrition, can 'power-pack' your meals and snacks, and further enhance your eating pattern.**"

Eating foods packed full of antioxidants is the best way to support your immune system. Now is the best time to look critically at your diet and to think about how you can improve it. You can start making superfoods a regular part of your daily diet.

For a list of superfoods see *Table 2*: **Love ♥ your superfoods!**

Love your superfoods!

This list is not exhaustive – there are simply too many superfoods – virtually all fruit and vegetables with bright colours – are superfoods.

Fruit & Berries	Cruciferous vegetables	Root vegetables	Herbs and Spices	Seeds	Wholegrains
Blueberries	Broccoli	Garlic	Ginger	Chia	Oats
Cranberries	Brussels	Sweet potato	Turmeric	Flax	Whole wheat
Goji berries	sprouts	Onion	Basil	Hemp	Bulgar wheat
Strawberries	Cabbage	Beetroot	Rosemary	Cocoa	Rye
Raspberries	Kale	Radish	Cinnamon	Coffee beans	Millet
Melon	Cauliflower	Turnip	Cloves	Sesame	Barley
Pineapple	Arugula	Fennel	Coriander	Pumpkin	Spelt
Kiwi fruit		Carrot	Dill	Sunflower	Quinoa
Avocado	**Leafy green**	Celeriac	Parsley		Brown rice
Pomegranate	**vegetables**		Chives		Corn
Pumpkin	Spinach				
Chilli peppers	Lettuce				
Tomatoes	Watercress				
Butternut	Endive				
squash					
Cucumber					

Nuts	Unsaturated oils	Fish e.g. oily fish	Meat	Legumes (peas/beans)	Other
Almonds	Olive oil	Salmon	Chicken	Soy	Honey
Walnuts	Sunflower oil	Sardines	Turkey	Mung	Bee pollen
Pistachio	Rapeseed oil	Mackerel		Cannellini	Algae e.g.
Brazils	Vegetable oil	(Any fish or	Lean cuts of;	Pinto	Spirulina,
Cashews		seafood is a	Beef	Black-eye	Chlorella
Hazelnuts	**Coconut oil	superfood)	Pork	Chickpeas	
	contains 86%		Lamb	Lentils	
	saturated fat	*Limit fish		Peanuts	
	– more than	containing	**Eggs**		
	butter – and	high levels of	Chicken egg		
	is not a	mercury e.g.	Duck egg		
	superfood!	swordfish,	Goose egg		
		shark and	Quail e.g.		
		fresh tuna			

*Mercury levels in fish 2019 FDA https://www.fda.gov/food/consumers/advice-about-eating-fish

** Is Coconut Oil A Superfood? - BBC https://www.bbc.co.uk/news/health-42608071

What You Need To Know About Superfoods - At A Glance:

1. **Steam Veggies In A Microwave**:

Don't over boil them. Roasting maintains nutrition but it can deteriorate with the length of cooking. Do not fry them or cover them with butter or salt!

https://www.myfooddiary.com/blog/healthiest-ways-to-cook-vegetables

2. **Fresh Produce:** Eat fresh when possible, however, there is excellent nutritional value eating fruit and vegetables, canned or frozen. However, look for products canned in water for example, with no added salt, and fruits in natural juice, with no added sugar.
https://www.ncbi.nlm.nih.gov/pmc/articles/PMC3649719/

3. **Check A Portion Size Guide**. For example - an average baked potato should be the size of your fist. One portion of fruit is one piece of fruit or one cupful of produce.
https://www.ncbi.nlm.nih.gov/pmc/articles/PMC3649719/

4. **No Fruit Juice.** The sugar content of fruit juices tends to be very high. Eat an orange instead! A lot of the nutrition – including the fibre - is in the pulp of the orange. This is also much more filling.

https://www.diabetes.org.uk/guide-to-diabetes/enjoy-food/what-to-drink-with-diabetes/fruit-juices-and-smoothies

5. **Raw Fruit And Vegetables** have the highest nutritional content.
https://www.medicalnewstoday.com/articles/7381

6. **Buy Organic?** - Although there may be advantages to buying organic foods, a huge review of the literature looking at over 50,000 studies failed to confirm a nutritional benefit from organic food. Undoubtedly there are ethical and holistic reasons to support organic farming. However, at the moment it's beyond everybody's pocket. Try to buy local produce which has not had far to travel, store it properly and wash well before use.

https://academic.oup.com/ajcn/article/90/3/680/4597089

7. **Benefits Of Milk.** Many people believe cow's milk is a superfood. It contains large quantities of conjugated linoleic acid – a healthy trans fat (as opposed to unhealthy industrial produced trans fats) with powerful anti-oxidant properties. Also, Vitamin A, vitamin E and co-enzyme Q.

https://milkgenomics.org/article/ultimate-superfood-milk-offers-glass-full-antioxidants/

Plant-based milks offer similar nutritional content but don't score so well on taste. It's counterproductive to switch from cow's milk and then need to add sugar to your milk to make it palatable!

https://www.health.harvard.edu/staying-healthy/plant-milk-or-cows-milk-which-is-better-for-you

8. **Chicken Is A Superfood** – a good quality chicken breast contains more protein than beef and much less fat. It does not contain carbohydrates, trans-fats and is low in salt. Try substituting red meat for chicken in your diet.

https://www.chicken.ca/health/v/new-study-confirms-chicken-as-the-latest-superfood

9. **You Will Feel Full After Meals** if you: choose more protein, eat slowly and chew your food, drink water with meals, and don't eat in front of the TV – because being distracted takes your mind off what you are doing. Always have a large portion of low-density superfoods foods on your plate – fruit and vegetables – to fill you up.

10. **Eat Soup!** - Many studies have shown soup is an excellent way to fill you up, reduce overall calorie intake and eat more superfoods! Have a go at making your own?

https://www.ncbi.nlm.nih.gov/pmc/articles/PMC2128765/

Superfoods List

What are the superfoods? Take a look at *Table 2* - **Love Your Superfoods**

It's impossible to list all the superfoods! I've had to pick out just a few. Here's a summary below:

Fruits And Berries

Fruits are full of antioxidants, vitamins and minerals, natural sugars and fibre. All fruits and berries are superfoods.

Blueberries are packed with phytonutrients. Their bright colour is due to anthocyanin pigments - flavonoids with potent anti-inflammatory and antioxidant properties.

A 2020 review in the *Journal of Advanced Nutrition* reported regularly eating blueberries is associated with a lower risk of cardiovascular disease, type 2 diabetes, and death. They also help with weight management.

Cranberries are unique in that they contain A-type proanthocyanidin (PAC), which has mild antibacterial effects. Cranberry juice has been used in women with urinary tract infections, although the medical benefits are unproven. American cranberries are rich in polyphenols, which also have antioxidant, and anti-carcinogenic properties. Eating cranberries have shown favourable effects on blood pressure, cholesterol and arterial wall function, although this has not been so far, been proven to reduce the overall risk of heart disease.

Goji berries are bright orange or red berries found in Asia. They are often dried and made into soups, herbal teas, wine or juice. They are full of carotenoids, and flavonoids which are powerful antioxidants. They may help protect the retina in patients with diabetic retinopathy. Rats, fed Gogi berry extract for 10 days, had significantly lower blood glucose levels. Moreover, Gogi berries support body defence mechanisms and may slow the growth of cancer cells.

Strawberries contain ellagic acid, and flavonoids such as anthocyanin, catechin, quercetin and kaempferol. They are highly potent antioxidants. Strawberries have positive effects on the cardiovascular system and lipids. For example - In a 2008 study of patients with cardiovascular risk factors, strawberry puree, eaten along with other berries, was shown to significantly increase HDL cholesterol and lower blood pressure. In a 2010 randomised controlled trial, 30 obese subjects with metabolic syndrome were randomised to eat strawberries - either 50 g freeze-dried strawberries or 3 cups fresh strawberries per day - or drink 4 cups of water (control group), for 8 weeks. Those in the strawberry group demonstrated significantly lower levels of LDL cholesterol.

Chili Peppers – Did you know these are actually fruits? Capsaicin is the major ingredient of chilli. A 2017 study in the journal *PLOS one* surveyed the dietary intake of red hot chilli pepper in 16,719 participants. The authors found mortality was reduced by 13 % in those who regularly ate red hot chilli peppers. Although the reasons for this are not well understood, it is thought that capsaicin results in increased fat breakdown, promote heat production and facilitates weight loss. It also has antibacterial properties within the gut as well as potent anti-tumour effects.

Cruciferous Vegetables

Love your sprouts! Many people grimace when asked to eat sprouts – but they are vegetables which do you the world of good! Kale, cauliflower, broccoli and sprouts contain chemical compounds – called glucosinolates - which are toxic to early cancer cells. Sorry folks - American dietary guidelines do currently recommend regular consumption of these leafy, green vegetables!

Root Vegetables

Let's consider garlic, for example:-

Garlic – A bulb of garlic contains fibre, lipids, and vitamins A and C, but also two specific sulphur compounds. When a bulb of garlic is crushed it releases a sulphur compound called alliin. This is activated by the enzyme allynase to produce allicin. It is allicin which gives garlic it's characteristic smell and taste. Garlic has been shown to lower blood pressure, reduce cholesterol, increase fibrinolysis and may help reduce thrombosis (blood clots). In 1990 the US National Cancer Institute stated, 'garlic may be the most potent food to have anti-cancer preventative properties.'

Spices

Ginger and turmeric are superfoods of specific interest: **Ginger** – This rhizome is traditionally used in Chinese herbal medicine. It contains a wide range of compounds beneficial to health. The unique taste of ginger comes from the presence of sesquiterpene and monoterpenoid hydrocarbons. Ginger has major anti-inflammatory properties. It's a potent inhibitor of oxidative stress, and has protective effects on the cardiovascular system, and for diabetes and cancer. It can reduce nausea and vomiting, and also prevent muscle pain after exercise.

Turmeric - Also a rhizome and from the ginger family, turmeric contains curcumin, a polyphenol which has strong antioxidant and anti-inflammatory properties. It has a potent action to counteract chronic inflammation. There are several studies in humans, supporting the beneficial effects of curcumin. For example, it's been shown to reduce the levels of pro-inflammatory cytokines. The effects are complex and far-reaching. however, research does suggest there may be a therapeutic role for curcumin in treating metabolic syndrome, arthritis, anxiety and high cholesterol.

Seeds Wholegrains, cocoa, nuts, legumes (beans), coffee beans and oils – most oils derive from seeds – make up the seed category. Seeds have been part of the palaeolithic – 'hunter-gatherer diet' for centuries. Historically these are people who lived off the land on a diet of fresh meat, plants and seeds – whatever they could forage. Nuts and seeds made up a quarter of the diet!

Seeds offer specific nutritional benefits. For example:

Chia seeds derive from the herbaceous plant *Salvia Hispanic* which produces a fruit containing tiny seeds - called Chia seeds. The American Dietetic Association classes Chia seeds as 'bioactive foods' – these are 'foods which have nutritional components which enhance, inhibit or modify, physiologic or metabolic functions' (Biesalski 2009). Chia seeds are often found in muesli, or as thickeners in milkshakes or soups. Chia seeds have a high ratio of omega-6 to omega-3 fatty acids. They are also full of protein phosphorus, calcium and magnesium, vitamins B1 and B2. They are potent antioxidants, with an Oxygen Radical Absorbance (ORAC) capacity the same as hazelnuts and prunes.

Flax Seeds are a food crop grown in the Canadian prairies. Flax seeds produce oil – linseed oil, which are a brownish-red in colour. They can be ground and made into flour. Flax seeds have a high content of ω-3 α-linolenic acid (an essential omega – 3 polyunsaturated fatty acid), fibre, and also lignans - which are plant-based estrogens. Flax seeds have strong antioxidant properties. They have health benefits for cardiovascular

disease, high blood pressure, cancer, osteoporosis, autoimmune diseases and more. They are also used by women to help reduce menopausal symptoms.

Hemp Seeds derive from the plant Cannabis sativa. There are two types of this plant – the first type is Marijuana which is well known to have psychoactive properties and is illegal. However, the second type does not have psychoactive properties and is safe to eat. Hemp seeds are full of micronutrients – they are high in protein - containing all nine essential amino acids – and are also high in fibre. They are of specific of interest because they have a high content of omega-3 and of omega- 6 fatty acids.

Cocoa – In fact, a cacao bean is a seed – not a bean! The beans of the Theobroma cacao tree – cocoa beans – are consumed as chocolate all around the world. Cacao is a superfood, but when it's made into chocolate, this contains high levels of saturated fat and sugar – exactly what we should not be eating! In an excellent 2011 review '**Cocoa, Chocolate and Human**

Health', published in the journal *Antioxidants and Redox Signalling*, the authors reported some fascinating findings. Cacao contains high levels of phenolic antioxidants such as flavonoids and procyanidins. The flavonoid epicatechin has favourable effects on the endothelium of blood vessel walls, primarily because of its effect to facilitate local production of nitric oxide. Dark chocolate contains 30%-70% cocoa solids, whereas milk chocolate only contains 7%-15%. Milk chocolate tends to have higher levels of saturated fat and sugar. Dark chocolate contains high levels of magnesium, important for protein synthesis. Also, copper, important for brain growth and development, and potassium, important for heart health.

Studies of how cacao affects the human immune system have not been conducted, however in rats and mice, cacao has been shown to modulate the acute immune response by reducing the production of TNF-α, reducing NO production from macrophages and modifying the neutrophil response in inflammation. https://www.ncbi.nlm.nih.gov/pmc/articles/PMC3671179/

In his book - Eat Chocolate, Lose Weight - Will Clover PhD, claims that eating dark chocolate 20 minutes before meals, and 5 minutes after, will curb your appetite by 50%!

Coffee - A coffee bean is actually a seed – not a bean! Coffee has been found to have significant antioxidant properties, antibacterial and anti-cancer properties. It contains a high concentration of plant phenols. A 2017 meta-analysis of 127 studies published in the *Annual Review of Nutrition* concluded that coffee was associated with a reduced incidence of breast, colon and prostate cancer, for example, as well as a reduction in cardiovascular disease and reduced overall mortality. However, there was

also a higher risk of stomach and lung cancer, and a possible detrimental effect on cholesterol, although the authors felt this was more likely to be influenced by smoking.

Whole Grains

A whole grain contains the endosperm, the germ and the bran. The outer portion is full of fibre, and the kernel in the centre is full of vitamins and minerals. During the refining process, the outer germ and bran are removed, leaving the endosperm only. This is why white flour has less nutritional content than wholemeal or brown flour. There is some evidence that regular consumption may reduce the risks of cardiovascular disease, type-2 diabetes, bowel, pancreatic and stomach cancers.

Nuts - A nut is in fact, a seed encased in a hard shell. Nuts have many characteristics which can benefit human health. In a 2017 review in the journal *Nutrients*, the authors reviewed the health benefits of a range of different nuts for humans. Nuts contain monounsaturated and polyunsaturated fatty acids, high levels of protein and fibre and are a good source of vitamins E and K. They are also full of the minerals copper, magnesium, potassium and selenium. They have potent antioxidant properties as they contain large amounts of carotenoids and other phytochemicals.

- **Almonds** – in one study of participants at high risk of type 2 diabetes, taking 43g per day of almonds as snacks throughout the day for 4 weeks, reduced the feeling of hunger and also blood glucose concentrations. Interestingly study subjects did not gain weight throughout the study.

  In a further study, eating 60 g of almonds per day for 10 weeks did not result in weight gain either!

- **Walnuts** may be useful in reducing visceral fat. High levels of visceral fat are associated with low concentrations of adiponectin – a hormone involved in regulating glucose levels and breaking down fat.

  In one small study, eating 48g walnuts per day for 4 days increased adiponectin levels by 15%, as well as showing significant improvements in their lipid profile.

- **Pistachios** have been shown to have health benefits for diabetics.

In one study, diabetics eating two snacks a day of 25 g pistachios, had a significant reduction in glycosylated haemoglobin (a marker of diabetic control) and fasting blood glucose.

Legumes are different types of beans. However, they are in the category of seeds because they are the fruits of plants that grow in pods. Beans are full of protein and fibre, rich in B vitamins, and minerals such as iron, copper, magnesium and zinc. A meta-analysis of ten prospective studies concluded that eating legumes for 3 weeks, significantly reduced total cholesterol and LDL cholesterol. Studies in diabetics have shown a regular intake of legumes can lower blood pressure and help improve blood sugars. Adults who regularly eat legumes have a lower body weight than those who do not. Legumes are an integral part of the Mediterranean Diet.

Olive Oil

Olive oil is a healthy, 'unsaturated' fat. It is extracted from olives by a process of crushing or pressing the fruit of the olive itself – not the seed in the middle. The refining process removes a lot of the fruit pulp from the oil but in doing so, also removes the potential health benefits. The most nutritious olive oil is unrefined - Extra Virgin Olive oil – which contains the highest concentration of polyphenols. 98-99% of olive oil is made up of triacylglycerols (TGA's). This is mostly monounsaturated oleic acid, but also palmitic, stearic and linoleic oils. It is packed full of other phytonutrients including phenolic acids, lignans and flavonoids.

The vast majority of studies about health and olive oil have been done in animals, but experts are confident many of these health benefits are seen in humans too. Olive oil has strong antioxidant properties. For example, polyphenols reduce levels of cytokines such as TNF-α, arachidonic acid, IL-6, NF-kB and PEG-2 – all markers of chronic inflammation. One of the key phenolic acids in olive oil is called hydroxytyrosol (HT), has been shown to stimulate mitochondrial biosynthesis, and may offer specific benefits to people with diabetes in whom mitochondrial synthesis is reduced.

Fish

Fish is an important part of a healthy diet, especially for your heart. It's a rich source of protein and omega-3 fatty acids (eicosapentaenoic acid (EPA) and docosahexaenoic acid (DH), vitamin D, iodine and selenium. Oily fish such as salmon, mackerel or sardines contain a particularly high concentration of omega-3 fatty acids. These are essential in the structure and maintenance of the cell wall. They also have a major role in the immune response, for example, to reduce the production of proinflammatory cytokines. They are also involved in fat storage and metabolism.

Omega-3 is most beneficial when obtained from the diet rather than tablet supplementation.

Vitamin D is formed naturally in the skin in sunlight. However, levels of vitamin D are often low especially in the winter when the days are short. Low vitamin D levels are associated with metabolic syndrome and obesity. Fish is the only other natural source of vitamin D.

Fish contains high levels of iodine and selenium - both essential for normal thyroid function. People with metabolic syndrome, tend to have higher thyroid volumes. American FDA guidelines recommend eating 8 oz of fish/shellfish, 2-3 times per week (2 -3 portions/week).

Egg - The humble egg has much to commend it! Egg contains large amounts of protein, for only a moderate number of calories, and is a rich source of Vitamin A, B12 and iron, zinc and calcium. Eggs are inexpensive and versatile. Egg contains high levels of antioxidants and for example, may reduce oxidative stress in the gut wall. Some of the egg constituents, for example, egg-white pleiotrophin, play a key role in the immune response, helping to prolong lymphocyte survival, and also by signalling white cells to move to the area of and immune attack (chemotaxis).

There has been concern about whether eating too many eggs might raise cholesterol. A very recent study published in the *Journal of the American*

Medical Association JAMA March 2020, showed that eating 3-4 eggs per week, as is currently recommended in the US, increased the risk of cardiovascular disease by 6% and death by 8%. However, before you get too worried about this, a major limitation of the study is that the investigators only ask people what they had been eating, from memory. This may well mean the results were not very accurate. The authors concluded people should not stop eating eggs, but eat them in moderation, and try to reduce cholesterol from their diet, for example by limiting red meat.

The Microbiome And The Immune System

Your gut contains 10 - 100 trillion micro-organisms! These are bacteria, viruses and fungi - which live in and around the lumen of your gut wall. Your body learns to recognise which cells belong to you, which ones can live there happily and which it needs to destroy. Each person on the planet has a different microbiome. At birth, the gut is almost sterile, but this is gradually colonised as the baby feeds by breast or bottle, and then by the introduction of solid food. Throughout life, everyone acquires a different gut flora according to their diet and health.

The constituents of your gut flora have a huge effect on your health. The organisms in the gut wall signal the brain to take specific actions. They also directly stimulate or switch off various biochemical processes. By analysing your faeces, scientists can analyse your microbiome. The constituents of your microbiome have a direct effect on the function of your immune system. However, you can make changes to your gut microbiome by making changes to your diet.

The Mediterranean Diet, for example, has been shown to result in alterations to the microbiome, and this is then associated with significant changes in markers of chronic inflammation. In a study published very recently (13th March 2020) in the *New England Journal of Medicine,* 612 frail elderly people were followed by for 12-months before, and then for 12 - months after, adopting the Mediterranean Diet.

After the study, the authors found a change in the diversity of organisms within the microbiome, along with an overall improvement in their levels of frailty, and improved cognitive function. They also found significant changes in markers of chronic inflammation such as C-reactive protein and interleukin -17.

There is much yet to be learned about the gut microbiome and its importance for human health. However one fact, which has been clearly established, it that the flora in the gut of an obese person is very different from that of someone who is lean. A comprehensive 2017 review, the authors concluded that making changes to your diet can indeed change your microbiome and result in improvements in health.

Final Thoughts

In this chapter, I've explained the importance of a healthy diet to maintain a healthy immune system and a healthy body. I hope you can see that improving your immune system is not just about eating an occasional apple or swallowing a vitamin pill! It's about improving your general health, and a large part of this comes down to improving your diet.

Remember that leanness is correlated with longevity. Don't we all want to live a long life? When did you last weigh and measure yourself and work out your BMI? If you are facing up to being obese – you are not alone. Isn't it time we all took responsibility for our health and did something about it? COVID-19 marks the time for change. Every situation is an opportunity.

We can all emerge from is pandemic healthier and happier if we try. Finding a diet that you can follow which is interesting, delicious and filling is one of nature's wonders. There are so many amazing things you can eat, recipes you can follow and fantastic food experiences that go far beyond reaching for another hot dog! I want you to stay well during this COVID-19 pandemic, and beyond!

So right now ... I'm off to fix myself a fruit smoothie!

Dr Deborah Lee

About the author

Sexual And Reproductive Health Specialist, Medical And Healthcare Writer
BM, MFFP, MRCGP, DRCOG, Dip GUM, Dip Colp, LOC Med Ed
GMC no. 3129913

Dr Deborah Lee has worked for many years in the NHS, mostly as Lead Clinician within an integrated Community Sexual Health Service. She now works as a health and medical writer, with an emphasis on women's health. Dr Lee is a medical content writer for Dr Fox (Dr Fox Online Pharmacy).

Dr Lee writes for many media outlets including **The Sun, The Daily Express, Bella magazine, Red magazine, Cosmopolitan, Net Doctor,** and many more. She remains passionate about all aspects of medicine - including obesity, weight loss, diet, and nutrition.

After qualifying from **University of Southampton** Medical School in 1986, Dr Lee trained as a GP and after a number of years specialised in Sexual & Reproductive Health (S&RH).

S&RH is a very broad speciality which includes for example: Gynaecology and Medical Gynaecology, all types and aspects of contraceptive care including coils and implants, dealing with unplanned pregnancies, abnormal smears, screening and treating STIs in both males and females, Young People's Sexual Health, Sexual Assault, and in particular Menopause Care - which has been her special interest. Dr Lee set up and ran her own specialist menopause clinic.

During this time, Dr Lee wrote extensively, and had numerous medical publications, as well as working as sub-editor for a medical journal. She has also written articles for The Huffington Post UK under the pseudonym Dr Daisy Mae.

Medical education and training has also been a large part of Dr Lee's professional career. She has been a Contraception & Sexual Health Trainer, a Faculty Examiner and a Training Programme Director.

Dr Deborah Lee/ Dr Daisy Mae

Freelance Health Writer https://healthcarewriterdr.com/services/

- **Dr Daisy's Sexual Health Blog, The Huffington Post**
  https://www.huffingtonpost.co.uk/author/daisy-mae/
- **Dr Daisy Blog, - Menopause Matters**
  https://www.menopausematters.co.uk/daisyblog.php
- **LinkedIn** - www.linkedin.com/in/dr-daisy-mae
- **Twitter- Daisy Mae**

References for Dr Deborah Lee's Chapter

For more information -
- Dietary Guidelines for Americans 2015-2020 – 8th Edition USDA https://health.gov/sites/default/files/2019-09/2015-2020_Dietary_Guidelines.pdf
- BMI calculator https://bmicalculatorusa.com/
- Find a Nutritionist https://www.nutritionistresource.org.uk/?gclid=CjwKCAjwssD0BRBIEiwA-JP5rLISdbdRqmgpNlZR_khFW5JuucRwD2pd8f8N7rzACwR8NqWLrG58ZBoC36QQAvD_BwE
- American Heart Association – Losing Weight https://www.heart.org/en/healthy-living/healthy-eating/losing-weight
- The Health Sciences Academy Free Starter Course Online https://thehealthsciencesacademy.org/registration-free-starter-nutrition-course/

....

References

Nutritional Modulation of Immune Function: Analysis of Evidence, Mechanisms, and Clinical Relevance. Front Immunol. 2018; 9: 3160. Published online 2019 Jan 15. doi: 10.3389/fimmu.2018.03160. PMCID: PMC6340979. PMID: 30697214 Nutritional Modulation of Immune Function: Analysis of Evidence, Mechanisms, and Clinical Relevance. Dayong Wu,1,* Erin D. Lewis,1 Munyong Pae,2 and Simin Nikbin Meydani1
https://www.ncbi.nlm.nih.gov/pmc/articles/PMC6340979/

Understanding nutrition and immunity in disease management. Journal of Traditional and Complementary Medicine. Volume 7, Issue 4, October 2017, Pages 386-391
Edwin L.Cooper, Melissa J.May. https://doi.org/10.1016/j.jtcme.2016.12.002
https://www.sciencedirect.com/science/article/pii/S2225411016303029

Gut barrier function in malnourished patients. Gut. 1998 Mar; 42(3): 396–401.doi: 10.1136/gut.42.3.396. PMCID: PMC1727047. PMID: 9577348. F Welsh, S Farmery, K MacLennan, M Sheridan, G Barclay, P Guillou, and J Reynolds
https://www.ncbi.nlm.nih.gov/pmc/articles/PMC1727047/

The Interaction between Nutrition and Infection. Peter Katona, Judit Katona-ApteClinical Infectious Diseases, Volume 46, Issue 10, 15 May 2008, Pages 1582–1588, https://doi.org/10.1086/587658 Published: 15 May 2008
https://academic.oup.com/cid/article/46/10/1582/294025

Feeding America https://www.feedingamerica.org/.
https://www.feedingamerica.org/hunger-in-america/facts

The Hidden Dangers of Fast and Processed Food. Am J Lifestyle Med. 2018 Sep-Oct; 12(5): 375–381. Published online 2018 Apr 3. doi: 10.1177/1559827618766483. PMCID: PMC6146358 PMID: 30283262. Joel Fuhrman, MD

Association of changes in red meat consumption with total and cause-specific mortality among US women and men: two prospective cohort studies. BMJ 2019; 365 doi: https://doi.org/10.1136/bmj.l2110 (Published 12 June 2019)Cite this as: BMJ 2019;365:l2110

What is a plant-based diet and why should you try it? POSTED SEPTEMBER 26, 2018, 10:30 AM, UPDATED SEPTEMBER 27, 2018, 12:56 PM Katherine D. McManus, MS, RD, LDN
https://www.health.harvard.edu/blog/what-is-a-plant-based-diet-and-why-should-you-try-it-2018092614760

Overweight and diabetes prevention: is a low-carbohydrate–high-fat diet recommendable? Eur J Nutr. 2018; 57(4): 1301–1312.Fred Brouns. Published online 2018 Mar 14. doi: 10.1007/s00394-018-1636-yPMCID: PMC5959976. PMID: 29541907
https://www.ncbi.nlm.nih.gov/pmc/articles/PMC5959976/

Fat: The Facts. NHS Eat Well https://www.nhs.uk/live-well/eat-well/different-fats-nutrition/

2 years of calorie restriction and cardiometabolic risk (CALERIE): exploratory outcomes of a multicentre, phase 2, randomised controlled trial. Kraus WE, et al Lancet Diabetes and Endocrinology. 2019 July 11. doi: 10.1016/S2213-8587(19)30151-2. [Epub ahead of print].

Does the Interdependence between Oxidative Stress and Inflammation Explain the Antioxidant Paradox? Oxid Med Cell Longev. 2016; 2016: 5698931. Published online 2016 Jan 5. doi: 10.1155/2016/5698931 PMCID: PMC4736408 PMID: 26881031. Subrata Kumar Biswas *

https://www.ncbi.nlm.nih.gov/pmc/articles/PMC4736408/

NHS Choices: What is the glycaemic index? https://www.nhs.uk/common-health-questions/food-and-diet/what-is-the-glycaemic-index-gi/

British Nutrition Foundation – Dietary Fibre
https://www.nutrition.org.uk/healthyliving/basics/fibre.html

World Health Organisation - Salt Reduction
https://www.who.int/news-room/fact-sheets/detail/salt-reduction

Harvard School of Public Health, The Healthy eating Plate -
https://www.hsph.harvard.edu/nutritionsource/healthy-eating-plate/

Mediterranean diet and life expectancy; beyond olive oil, fruits and vegetables. Curr Opin Clin Nutr Metab Care. Author manuscript; available in PMC 2018 Apr 17. Published in final edited form as: Curr Opin Clin Nutr Metab Care. 2016 Nov; 19(6): 401–407. doi: 10.1097/MCO.0000000000000316. PMCID: PMC5902736. NIHMSID: NIHMS939601 PMID: 27552476. Miguel A. Martinez-Gonzalez1,2 and Nerea Martín-Calvo1,2

https://www.ncbi.nlm.nih.gov/pmc/articles/PMC5902736/

Mediterranean Diet and Health Status: An Updated Meta-Analysis and a Proposal for a Literature-Based Adherence Score Public Health Nutr, 17 (12), 2769-82 Dec 2014
Francesco Sofi 1, Claudio Macchi 2, Rosanna Abbate 1, Gian Franco Gensini 1, Alessandro Casini 1 PMID: 24476641 DOI: 10.1017/S1368980013003169

https://pubmed.ncbi.nlm.nih.gov/24476641/?dopt=Abstract

Dietary Patterns and Type 2 Diabetes: A Systematic Literature Review and Meta-Analysis of Prospective Studies Franziska Jannasch, Janine Kröger, Matthias B Schulze
The Journal of Nutrition, Volume 147, Issue 6, June 2017, Pages 1174–1182,
https://doi.org/10.3945/jn.116.242552 Published: 19 April 2017
https://academic.oup.com/jn/article/147/6/1174/4630426?ijkey=bb2d628650e989a9a4cdcb6512fe189d503f5fc5&keytype2=tf_ipsecsha

Adherence to a Vegetarian Diet and Diabetes Risk: A Systematic Review and Meta-Analysis of Observational Studies by Yujin Lee and Kyong Park Department of Food and Nutrition, Yeungnam University, Gyeongsan 38541, Gyeongbuk, Korea. Nutrients 2017, 9(6), 603; https://doi.org/10.3390/nu9060603. Received: 11 May 2017 / Revised: 7 June 2017 / Accepted: 10 June 2017 / Published: 14 June 2017

https://www.mdpi.com/2072-6643/9/6/603/htm

Top Trends in Prepared Foods 2017: Exploring trends in meat, fish and seafood; pasta, noodles and rice; prepared meals; savory deli food; soup; and meat substitutes. June 2017 Report ID: 4959853 • Format: PDF https://www.reportbuyer.com/product/4959853/top-

trends-in-prepared-foods-2017-exploring-trends-in-meat-fish-and-seafood-pasta-noodles-and-rice-prepared-meals-savory-deli-food-soup-and-meat-substitutes.html
The Vegan Society   https://www.vegansociety.com/news/media/statistics

Effect of the Anti-Inflammatory Diet in People with Diabetes and Pre-Diabetes: A Randomized Controlled Feeding Study. J Restor Med. Author manuscript; available in PMC 2019 Jun 5.
Published in final edited form as: J Restor Med. 2019; 8(1): e20190107.
Published online 2019 Feb 15. doi: 10.14200/jrm.2019.0107 PMCID: PMC6550471
NIHMSID: NIHMS1020614 PMID: 31179163 . Heather Zwickey, PhD, a,* Angela Horgan, PhD, RD, LD,b Doug Hanes, PhD, a Heather Schiffke, MATCM, Annie Moore, MD, MBA,c Helané Wahbeh, ND, MCR, a Julia Jordan, MS, RD, LD,b Lila Ojeda, MS, RDN,b Martha McMurry,b Patricia Elmer, PhD, a,§ and Jonathan Q Purnell, MDb
https://www.ncbi.nlm.nih.gov/pmc/articles/PMC6550471/

American Institute for Cancer Research. About the Third Expert Report. Diet, Nutrition, Physical Activity and Cancer: a Global Perspective.
https://www.wcrf.org/sites/default/files/Meat-Fish-and-Dairy-products.pdf

Vitamin C and Immune Function Nutrients. 2017 Nov; 9(11): 1211. Published online 2017 Nov 3. doi: 10.3390/nu9111211. PMCID: PMC5707683. PMID: 29099763. Anitra C. Carr1,* and Silvia Maggini2 https://www.ncbi.nlm.nih.gov/pmc/articles/PMC5707683

The effects of plant-based diets on the body and the brain: a systematic review. Transl Psychiatry. 2019; 9: 226. Published online 2019 Sep 12. doi: 10.1038/s41398-019-0552-0
PMCID: PMC6742661 PMID: 31515473. Evelyn Medawar, 1,2,3 Sebastian Huhn,4 Arno Villringer,1,2,3 and A. Veronica Witte1
https://www.ncbi.nlm.nih.gov/pmc/articles/PMC6742661/#CR57

British Nutrition Society – Protein https://www.nutrition.org.uk/nutritionscience/nutrients-food-and-ingredients/protein.html?start=2
Effects of Superfoods on Risk Factors of Metabolic Syndrome: A Systematic Review of Human Intervention Trials José J van den Driessche 1, Jogchum Plat 1, Ronald P Mensink 1 PMID: 29557436 DOI: 10.1039/C7FO01792H
https://pubmed.ncbi.nlm.nih.gov/29557436/
Cranberries

Cranberries and Their Bioactive Constituents in Human Health1,2. Adv Nutr. 2013 Nov; 4(6): 618–632. Published online 2013 Nov 6. doi: 10.3945/an.113.004473PMCID: PMC3823508 PMID: 24228191. Jeffrey B. Blumberg,3,* Terri A. Camesano,4 Aedin Cassidy,5 Penny Kris-Etherton,6 Amy Howell,7 Claudine Manach,8 Luisa M. Ostertag,5 Helmut Sies,9 Ann Skulas-Ray,6 and Joseph A. Vita10 https://www.ncbi.nlm.nih.gov/pmc/articles/PMC3823508/

Blueberries

Recent Research on the Health Benefits of Blueberries and Their Anthocyanins Adv Nutr,11 (2), 224-236, 2020 Mar 1 Wilhelmina Kalt 1, Aedin Cassidy 2, Luke R Howard 3, Robert Krikorian 4, April J Stull 5, Francois Tremblay 6, Raul Zamora-Ros 7 Affiliations expand PMID: 31329250 DOI: 10.1093/advances/nmz065 https://pubmed.ncbi.nlm.nih.gov/31329250/

Gogi berries

Goji Berries as a Potential Natural Antioxidant Medicine: An Insight into Their Molecular Mechanisms of Action. Oxid Med Cell Longev. 2019; 2019: 2437397. Published online 2019 Jan 9. doi: 10.1155/2019/2437397 PMCID: PMC6343173 PMID: 30728882. Zheng Feei Ma, 1, 2 Hongxia Zhang, 3 Sue Siang Teh, 3, 4 Chee Woon Wang, 5 Yutong Zhang, 6 Frank Hayford, 7 Liuyi Wang, 1 Tong Ma, 8 Zihan Dong, 1 Yan Zhang, 1 and Yifan Zhu 1 https://www.ncbi.nlm.nih.gov/pmc/articles/PMC6343173/

Strawberries

Favorable Effects of Berry Consumption on Platelet Function, Blood Pressure, and HDL Cholesterol. Randomised Controlled Trial. Am J Clin Nutr, 87 (2), 323-31 Feb 2008. Iris Erlund 1, Raika Koli, Georg Alfthan, Jukka Marniemi, Pauli Puukka, Pirjo Mustonen, Pirjo Mattila, Antti Jula. PMID: 18258621 DOI: 10.1093/ajcn/87.2.323 https://pubmed.ncbi.nlm.nih.gov/18258621/

Strawberries 2

Strawberries decrease atherosclerotic markers in subjects with metabolic syndrome. Nutr Res. Author manuscript; available in PMC 2011 Jul 1. Published in final edited form as: Nutr Res. 2010 Jul; 30(7): 462–469. doi: 10.1016/j.nutres.2010.06.016 PMCID: PMC2929388 NIHMSID: NIHMS223632 PMID: 20797478 Arpita Basu,* Mei Du,# Marci Wilkinson,* Brandi Simmons,* Mingyuan Wu,# Nancy M. Betts,* Dong Xu Fu,# and Timothy J. Lyons#† https://www.ncbi.nlm.nih.gov/pmc/articles/PMC2929388/#R5

Chilli

The Association of Hot Red Chili Pepper Consumption and Mortality: A Large Population-Based Cohort Study. PLoS One. 2017; 12(1): e0169876. Published online 2017 Jan 9. doi: 10.1371/journal.pone.0169876 PMCID: PMC5222470 PMID: 28068423 Mustafa Chopan*

and Benjamin Littenberg Oreste Gualillo, Editor
https://www.ncbi.nlm.nih.gov/pmc/articles/PMC5222470/

Garlic

Garlic: a review of potential therapeutic effects. Avicenna J Phytomed. 2014 Jan-Feb; 4(1): 1–14. PMCID: PMC4103721 PMID: 25050296. Leyla Bayan,1 Peir Hossain Koulivand,1 and Ali Gorji1,2,* https://www.ncbi.nlm.nih.gov/pmc/articles/PMC4103721/#B22

Ginger

Anti-Oxidative and Anti-Inflammatory Effects of Ginger in Health and Physical Activity: Review of Current Evidence. Int J Prev Med. 2013 Apr; 4(Suppl 1): S36–S42. PMCID: PMC3665023 PMID: 23717767. Nafiseh Shokri Mashhadi, Reza Ghiasvand,1,2 Gholamreza Askari,1,2 Mitra Hariri,1,2 Leila Darvishi,1,2 and Mohammad Reza Mofid3
https://www.ncbi.nlm.nih.gov/pmc/articles/PMC3665023/

Chia seeds

The Chemical Composition and Nutritional Value of Chia Seeds—Current State of Knowledge. Nutrients. 2019 Jun; 11(6): 1242. Published online 2019 May 31. doi: 10.3390/nu11061242. PMCID: PMC6627181 PMID: 31159190. Bartosz Kulczyński,1 Joanna Kobus-Cisowska,1 Maciej Taczanowski,2 Dominik Kmiecik,1 and Anna Gramza-Michałowska1,*

https://www.ncbi.nlm.nih.gov/pmc/articles/PMC6627181/

Flax seeds

Flax and flaxseed oil: an ancient medicine & modern functional food. J Food Sci Technol. 2014 Sep; 51(9): 1633–1653. Published online 2014 Jan 10. doi: 10.1007/s13197-013-1247-9

PMCID: PMC4152533. PMID: 25190822. Ankit Goyal, Vivek Sharma, Neelam Upadhyay, Sandeep Gill, and Manvesh Sihag
https://www.ncbi.nlm.nih.gov/pmc/articles/PMC4152533/

Quinoa

Quinoa Seed Lowers Serum Triglycerides in Overweight and Obese Subjects: A Dose-Response Randomized Controlled Clinical Trial. Curr Dev Nutr. 2017 Sep; 1(9): e001321. Published online 2017 Aug 24. doi: 10.3945/cdn.117.001321

PMCID: PMC5998774. PMID: 29955719. Diana Navarro-Perez,1 Jessica Radcliffe,2 Audrey Tierney,2 and Markandeya Jois1
https://www.ncbi.nlm.nih.gov/pmc/articles/PMC5998774/#b3

Cocoa

Cocoa and Chocolate in Human Health and Disease. Antioxid Redox Signal. 2011 Nov 15; 15(10): 2779–2811. doi: 10.1089/ars.2010.3697. MCID: PMC4696435. PMID: 21470061
David L. Katz, Kim Doughty, and Ather Ali
https://www.ncbi.nlm.nih.gov/pmc/articles/PMC4696435/#B149

National Centre for Complementary and Integrative Health – Acai.
https://www.nccih.nih.gov/health/acai

United States Department of Agriculture – Industrial Hemp. https://nifa.usda.gov/industrial-hemp

Nuts

Nuts and Human Health Outcomes: A Systematic Review. Nutrients. 2017 Dec; 9(12): 1311. Published online 2017 Dec 2. doi: 10.3390/nu9121311. PMCID: PMC5748761. PMID: 29207471 Rávila Graziany Machado de Souza, Raquel Machado Schincaglia, Gustavo Duarte Pimentel, and João Felipe Mota*.
https://www.ncbi.nlm.nih.gov/pmc/articles/PMC5748761/

Fish

Nutrients in Fish and Possible Associations with Cardiovascular Disease Risk Factors in Metabolic Syndrome. Nutrients. 2018 Jul; 10(7): 952. Published online 2018 Jul 23. doi: 10.3390/nu10070952 PMCID: PMC6073188. PMID: 30041496 Christine Tørris,1,* Milada Cvancarova Småstuen,1 and Marianne Molin1,2
https://www.ncbi.nlm.nih.gov/pmc/articles/PMC6073188/#B88-nutrients-10-00952

Olive oil

Potential Health Benefits of Olive Oil and Plant Polyphenols. Int J Mol Sci. 2018 Mar; 19(3): 686. Published online 2018 Feb 28. doi: 10.3390/ijms19030686. PMCID: PMC5877547. PMID: 29495598. Monika Gorzynik-Debicka,1,† Paulina Przychodzen,1,† Francesco Cappello,2,3 Alicja Kuban-Jankowska,1 Antonella Marino Gammazza,2,3 Narcyz Knap,1 Michal Wozniak,1 and Magdalena Gorska-Ponikowska1,4,*
https://www.ncbi.nlm.nih.gov/pmc/articles/PMC5877547/

Food

Feeding the Immune System. Proc Nutr Soc. 72 (3), 299-309 Aug 2013 Philip C Calder 1
PMID: 23688939.DOI: 10.1017/S0029665113001286
https://pubmed.ncbi.nlm.nih.gov/23688939/

Whole grains

Health Benefits of Dietary Whole Grains: An Umbrella Review of Meta-analyses. J Chiropr Med. 2017 Mar; 16(1): 10–18. Published online 2016 Nov 18. doi: 10.1016/j.jcm.2016.08.008
PMCID: PMC5310957 PMID: 28228693. Marc P. McRae, MSc, DC, FACN, DACBN∗
https://www.ncbi.nlm.nih.gov/pmc/articles/PMC5310957/

Recommending superfoods. Harvard Medical School. 10 superfoods to boost a healthy diet. POSTED AUGUST 29, 2018, 10:30 AM. Katherine D. McManus, MS, RD, LDN
https://www.health.harvard.edu/blog/10-superfoods-to-boost-a-healthy-diet-2018082914463

Turmeric

Curcumin: A Review of Its' Effects on Human Health. Foods. 2017 Oct; 6(10): 92. Published online 2017 Oct 22. doi: 10.3390/foods6100092. PMCID: PMC5664031. PMID: 29065496. Susan J. Hewlings1,2,* and Douglas S. Kalman3,4
https://www.ncbi.nlm.nih.gov/pmc/articles/PMC5664031/#B29-foods-06-00092

Ginger

Anti-Oxidative and Anti-Inflammatory Effects of Ginger in Health and Physical Activity: Review of Current Evidence. Int J Prev Med. 2013 Apr; 4(Suppl 1): S36–S42...PMCID: PMC3665023. PMID: 23717767. Nafiseh Shokri Mashhadi, Reza Ghiasvand,1,2 Gholamreza Askari,1,2 Mitra Hariri,1,2 Leila Darvishi,1,2 and Mohammad Reza Mofid3
https://www.ncbi.nlm.nih.gov/pmc/articles/PMC3665023/

Health benefits of seeds

Consumption of Plant Seeds and Cardiovascular Health: Epidemiologic and Clinical Trial Evidence. Circulation. Author manuscript; available in PMC 2014 Jul 30.
Published in final edited form as: Circulation. 2013 Jul 30; 128(5): 553–565.

doi: 10.1161/CIRCULATIONAHA.112.001119. PMCID: PMC3745769. NIHMSID: NIHMS510316. PMID: 23897849. Emilio Ros, MD, PhD1 and Frank B. Hu, MD, PhD2
https://www.ncbi.nlm.nih.gov/pmc/articles/PMC3745769/

Legumes: Health Benefits and Culinary Approaches to Increase Intake. Clin Diabetes. 2015 Oct; 33(4): 198–205. doi: 10.2337/diaclin.33.4.198 PMCID: PMC4608274. PMID: 26487796 Rani Polak, 1 Edward M. Phillips,1 and Amy Campbell2
https://www.ncbi.nlm.nih.gov/pmc/articles/PMC4608274/

Coffee

Coffee, Caffeine, and Health Outcomes: An Umbrella Review. Annual Review of Nutrition. Vol. 37:131-156 (Volume publication date August 2017) Giuseppe Grosso,1,2 Justyna Godos,1,3 Fabio Galvano,3 and Edward L. Giovannucci4,5,6
https://www.annualreviews.org/doi/10.1146/annurev-nutr-071816-064941

Cruciferous vegetables

National Cancer Institute. Cruciferous Vegetables and Cancer Prevention
https://www.cancer.gov/about-cancer/causes-prevention/risk/diet/cruciferous-vegetables-fact-sheet

Egg

The Golden Egg: Nutritional Value, Bioactivities, and Emerging Benefits for Human Health. Nutrients. 2019 Mar; 11(3): 684. Published online 2019 Mar 22. doi: 10.3390/nu11030684. PMCID: PMC6470839. PMID: 30909449. Sophie Réhault-Godbert,* Nicolas Guyot, and Yves Nys. https://www.ncbi.nlm.nih.gov/pmc/articles/PMC6470839/

Northwestern University. "Higher egg and cholesterol consumption hikes heart disease and early death risk." ScienceDaily. ScienceDaily, 15 March 2019.
www.sciencedaily.com/releases/2019/03/190315110858.htm

Egg

Associations of Dietary Cholesterol or Egg Consumption with Incident Cardiovascular Disease and Mortality. March 19, 2019. Victor W. Zhong, PhD1; Linda Van Horn, PhD1; Marilyn C. Cornelis, PhD1; et al https://jamanetwork.com/journals/jama/fullarticle/2728487

The Microbiome

Defining the human microbiome, Luke K Ursell, Jessica L Metcalf, Laura Wegener Parfrey, Rob Knight. Nutrition Reviews, Volume 70, Issue suppl_1, 1 August 2012, Pages S38–S44, https://doi.org/10.1111/j.1753-4887.2012.00493.x Published: 01 August 2012* PMCID: PMC3426293. NIHMSID: NIHMS369735.. PMID: 22861806
https://academic.oup.com/nutritionreviews/article/70/suppl_1/S38/1921538

Microbiome in Mediterranean Diet

Ghosh TS, Rampelli S, Jeffery IB, et al. Mediterranean diet intervention alters the gut microbiome in older people reducing frailty and improving health status: the NU-AGE 1-year dietary intervention across five European countries. Gut Published Online First: 17 February 2020. doi: 10.1136/gutjnl-2019-319654.
https://gut.bmj.com/content/early/2020/01/31/gutjnl-2019-319654

The microbiome

20 Things You Didn't Know About the Human Gut Microbiome. J Cardiovasc Nurs. Author manuscript; available in PMC 2015 Nov 1. Published in final edited form as: J Cardiovasc Nurs. 2014 Nov-Dec; 29(6): 479–481. doi: 10.1097/JCN.0000000000000166. PMCID: PMC4191858. NIHMSID: NIHMS589935. PMID: 25290618
https://www.ncbi.nlm.nih.gov/pmc/articles/PMC4191858/

Influence of diet on the gut microbiome and implications for human health. J Transl Med. 2017; 15: 73. Published online 2017 Apr 8. doi: 10.1186/s12967-017-1175-y PMCID: PMC5385025. PMID: 28388917. Rasnik K. Singh,1 Hsin-Wen Chang,2 Di Yan,2 Kristina M. Lee,2 Derya Ucmak,2 Kirsten Wong,2 Michael Abrouk,3 Benjamin Farahnik,4 Mio Nakamura,2 Tian Hao Zhu,5 Tina Bhutani,2 and Wilson Liao 2
https://www.ncbi.nlm.nih.gov/pmc/articles/PMC5385025/

Studies don't show benefit from antioxidant tablets

Does the Interdependence between Oxidative Stress and Inflammation Explain the Antioxidant Paradox? Oxid Med Cell Longev. 2016; 2016: 5698931. Published online 2016 Jan 5. doi: 10.1155/2016/5698931 PMCID: PMC4736408 PMID: 26881031. Subrata Kumar Biswas https://www.ncbi.nlm.nih.gov/pmc/articles/PMC4736408/

Benefits of the Mediterranean Diet

Mediterranean Diet and Health Status: An Updated Meta-Analysis and a Proposal for a Literature-Based Adherence Score. Francesco Sofi 1, Claudio Macchi 2, Rosanna Abbate 1, Gian Franco Gensini 1, Alessandro Casini 1 PMID: 24476641 DOI: 10.1017/S1368980013003169 https://pubmed.ncbi.nlm.nih.gov/24476641/?dopt=Abstract

Effects of the plant-based diet

The effects of plant-based diets on the body and the brain: a systematic review. Transl Psychiatry. 2019; 9: 226. Published online 2019 Sep 12. doi: 10.1038/s41398-019-0552-0. PMCID: PMC6742661. PMID: 31515473. Evelyn Medawar, 1,2,3 Sebastian Huhn,4 Arno Villringer,1,2,3 and A. Veronica Witte1
https://www.ncbi.nlm.nih.gov/pmc/articles/PMC6742661/#CR57

Printed in Poland
by Amazon Fulfillment
Poland Sp. z o.o., Wrocław